PRAISE FO

MW00647306

"Pema Tseden is known internationally as an award-winning filmmaker, the elegant and contemplative pioneering auteur of new Tibetan cinema. Western audiences may not, however, be aware that he began his career as a critically acclaimed writer of short stories. Patricia Schiaffini-Vedani and Michael Monhart have, for the first time, shared with the English reader a comprehensive anthology of both his Chinese and Tibetan stories. The stories in this collection reflect Pema Tseden's characteristically observant, unhurried, and humanistic take on the violent social changes faced by Tibetans living at the edge of China's economic transformation. Schiaffini-Vedani and Monhart's translations are rich and faithful to the original texts. They must be commended for providing us with a valuable new source on cultural life in contemporary Tibet."

— Tsering Shakya, author of *The Dragon in the Land of Snows: A History of Modern Tibet Since 1947*

"Pema Tseden is the singularly most influential Tibetan filmmaker on the international scene. With this skillfully translated collection of short stories, *Enticement*, readers can now also appreciate his written works, including the renowned 'Tharlo.' In literary long shots, the author transforms grasslands, snowy expanses, and county seats into mindscapes with a curious and chilly brilliance until they are rendered translucent. Elsewhere, he racks focus with wry humor from quirky details to complex social realities, finding possibility in fantasy, chance meetings, and even mistranslation. Interspersed with the winsome and arboreal artwork of Wu Yao and with the orientation of an insightful introduction and preface, these contemporary tales beckon readers with all the promise of the title-story towards the liminal, where cultural and temporal displacement may point to new meanings."

— Lauran R. Hartley, Columbia University

"Pema Tseden, a distinguished writer and filmmaker, is an important leader among Tibetan intellectuals. He sees Tibet as more than a land of startling natural beauty, of profound religious heritage, and of galling colonization by the Communist Party of China—correct though those views are. For him, Tibetan culture lives not only in Tibet proper, but across Qinghai, Sichuan, and Gansu as well, and Tibetan people are not mystical Others but ordinary human beings (flawed, as we all are) who struggle to adapt their inherited lives to the modern world (as people everywhere, now or recently, have done). By looking beyond clichéd concepts to examine actual lives, Pema Tseden's work enriches Tibetan culture and shows a new face for it."

— Perry Link, author of *An Anatomy of Chinese:*
Rhythm, Metaphor, Politics

"For the first time in the Anglophone world, we have an extraordinary translation of short stories by the celebrated Tibetan filmmaker and writer Pema Tseden, originally written in Tibetan and Mandarin Chinese. While he wrote his stories in Tibetan for his Tibetan readers, in Mandarin Chinese for Chinese readers, the translators have brought both sets of stories together in one volume to allow readers to compare and contrast how he writes for different audiences. These stories, told in beguilingly simple and direct prose, are powerful vignettes of Tibetan life, as powerful as his deeply evocative films, filled not only with despair and loss but also beauty and longing. These elegant stories are almost more powerful in what they do not say than in what they do say. I recommend *Enticement* to everyone."

— Shu-mei Shih, author of *Visuality and Identity:*
Sinophone Articulations across the Pacific

"The blinding sun, wind storms, wolves, and death are at work in these vital and unforgettable stories. Equally, the social forces of surveillance, bureaucracy, information, misinformation, and romance propel the narratives, which encompass the ordinary and the truly strange. The collection is invaluable for offering an all too rare 'Tibetan view of Tibet,' revealing unexpected and disorienting perspectives on Buddhism and on Tibetans' engagements with the Chinese state. The characters we get to know are police officers, herders, artists, children, lamas, and lovers. They are all painfully and vividly alive, their every move and impulse represented with startlingly detailed observation. Readers will be richer in knowledge and imagination from spending time with these stories, so expertly translated that we feel we hear the author's compassionate and yet relentlessly perceptive voice. One is left with an impression that is crystal clear and yet uncanny. It is difficult to say whether the strongest draw of the stories is humor or sorrow."

— Dominique Townsend, Bard College

ENTICEMENT

དགེ་བ་ཅན་གྱི་ཆུ་ཆུ་ལ་སྐུལ་མ་གཏབ་པ།

སྐུ་ཆོ་ཅན་དུ་རསྨ།

20 18. 10. 6.

ENTICEMENT
STORIES OF TIBET

PEMA TSEDEN

Edited and translated by
Patricia Schiaffini-Vedani and Michael Monhart

with translations by
Françoise Robin and Carl Robertson

Cover art, Wu Yao, *Wish-fulfilling Tree Series, III*

Published by State University of New York Press, Albany

© 2018 State University of New York

All rights reserved

Printed in the United States of America

Book design, Aimee Harrison

For information, contact State University of New York Press
Albany, NY
www.sunypress.edu

Library of Congress Cataloging-in-Publication Data

Names: Pema Tseden, author.
Title: Enticement : stories of Tibet / Pema Tseden ; English translation
    by Patricia Schiaffini-Vedani and Michael Monhart.
Description: Albany, NY : State University of New York, 2018.
Identifiers: ISBN 9781438474267 (paperback : alk. paper) | ISBN
    9781438474274 (e-book)
Further information is available at the Library of Congress.

10 9 8 7 6 5 4 3 2 1

TRANSLATOR'S INTRODUCTION

— PATRICIA SCHIAFFINI-VEDANI

This book is the first English-language anthology of short stories by one of Tibet's most prominent writers and filmmakers, Pema Tseden. This collection includes stories originally written either in Tibetan or in Chinese. Pema Tseden's unique bilingual literary background is not common among Tibetan intellectuals, who tend to favor Tibetan, Chinese, or English, depending on their educational background. Since China began annexing Tibetan areas in the 1950s, Tibetan language has been taught on and off according to the prevalent political winds blowing from Beijing. The Tibetan writers who were fortunate enough to grow up in areas where Tibetan was still taught are nowadays able to write in their native language, while many other Tibetan writers can only write in Chinese, the language in which they were schooled in China, or in other languages if they grew up in exile.

Pema Tseden (b. 1969), born in Trika County (Qinghai Province, PRC), is one of those Tibetans who received a predominantly Tibetan-language education, despite having been born during the Cultural Revolution. His closeness to his grandfather, whose Buddhist practice included extensive reading of Tibetan-language religious texts, also played a part in Pema Tseden's familiarity with the Tibetan written language.* He

---

* I am very grateful to Françoise Robin for pointing out the closeness of Pema Tseden to his grandfather, and how his grandfather's passion for reading Tibetan-language Buddhist texts influenced Pema Tseden in his own quest to master Tibetan. Interestingly, the presence of a highly literate religious elder in the family, the mention of a grandfather that reads religious texts to a child, and personal

began his literary career both as a writer and as a translator of literature in the 1980s. After graduating from the Tsolho Nationalities' Normal College, where he continued learning Tibetan, and where he also studied Chinese, Pema Tseden worked as a teacher for several years in his hometown, but later on decided to continue his education at Lanzhou's Northwest Nationalities University. There he pursued undergraduate and graduate degrees in the Department of Tibetan Language and Literature, which is famous today for grooming young Tibetan intellectuals. At this time, he was already writing short stories in Chinese and Tibetan, and translating literature from both languages. To this day, Pema Tseden remains one of Tibet's most prolific translators. Contrary to many other Tibetan writers of his generation, he was never interested in poetry. It was his passion for fictional narratives and his disregard for poetry that preluded his later career as a successful filmmaker. In the 1990s, Pema Tseden was already fascinated with film, but such a career was almost unthinkable for a Tibetan. At that time, no Tibetans in China had ever studied or actively engaged in film directing or production. The closest Pema Tseden could get to creating an imaginary world of his own was writing short stories.

The relevance of Pema Tseden's short stories, films, and literary translations is intrinsically linked to his unique position as a bilingual and bicultural Tibetan intellectual. The conscious effort Pema Tseden made to master both Tibetan and Chinese languages paid off. He has been able to use his bilingualism and biculturalism to build a bridge between these two cultures, and to navigate the turbulent waters of censorship in China. Several compilations of his short stories, both in Chinese and Tibetan, have been published in China with much success. As he explains, "I often translate my own Tibetan-language stories into Chinese, but not necessarily word-by-word. I feel that sometimes I need to make small changes to make it more understandable for

---

attachment to specific sutras are present in some of the stories of this anthology, most clearly so in "Enticement" and "Afternoon."

Chinese audiences."[*] Pema Tseden's deep knowledge of both Tibetan and Chinese cultures allows him to portray Tibet from a Tibetan perspective to Chinese audiences who, for over fifty years, had been accustomed to patronizing, inaccurate, and politically-motivated Chinese renderings of Tibet. Pema Tseden's stories about Tibet have also captivated foreign audiences. His most popular short stories have been translated into English, French, German, Spanish, Japanese, Korean, and Czech, and anthologies of his works have recently been published in France and Japan.[†]

Pema Tseden's love of cinema and his resolution to become a filmmaker finally led him to the Beijing Film Academy. He was the first Tibetan to study there. From 2002 to 2004, he pursued non-degree studies in film directing, and in 2006, he went back to this prestigious institution to continue his studies in the same field, receiving his doctorate in 2009. He began his career in filmmaking in 2002 with short films and documentaries. Since then, he has released five major feature movies: *Silent Mani Stones* (2005), *The Search* (2009), *Old Dog* (2010), *Sacred Arrow* (2014), and *Tharlo* (2015), his first film based on one of his short stories, which is included in this anthology. His films have won prestigious awards in China, Japan, and Taiwan. Most recently, *Tharlo* was nominated for a Golden Lion at the 72nd Venice International Film Festival (September 2–12, 2015).

Some of the earliest artistic and literary influences for Pema Tseden were the Chinese translations of foreign literature that circulated in China in the 1980s, among them Kafka and García Márquez, but his works are also heavily influenced by traditional Tibetan culture and tales. The stories included in this anthology evoke a variety of

---

[*] Pema Tseden, personal interview, November 1, 2014.

[†] Pema Tseden, *Neige: nouvelles du Tibet*, trans. Françoise Robin and Brigitte Duzan (Arles: Philippe Picquier, 2012). Pad-ma-tshe-brtan, *Chibetto bungaku no genzai: Timē Kunden o sagashite*, trans. Izumi Hoshi and Kensaku Okawa (Tōkyō: Bensei Shuppan, 2013).

literary inspirations, such as magical realism, surrealism, and theater of the absurd. Without drama or surprise endings, and allowing readers freedom for interpretation, these stories provide a glimpse into the day-to-day negotiations between Tibetan traditional values and ways of life and those imposed by globalization, particularly the Chinese presence.

Beyond the influences of world literature, Pema Tseden's literary universe and style are very much linked to Tibetan oral storytelling. One of the most famous stories in traditional Tibetan oral literature, *Mi ro rtse sgrung* (*Tales of the Golden Corpse*), which Pema translated into Chinese, is the basis for his story "A New Golden Corpse Tale: Gun," included in this anthology. Cyclical plots, repetition of actions, and recurrence of words and grammatical structures appear constantly in his short stories. These techniques also feature prominently in his movies, through over-statement of concepts, repetition of the same reactions by different characters, and reiteration of similar shots. The rhythmic quality of reappearances and paraphrasing evoke the traditional oral Tibetan tales he listened to as a child.

As he has expressed in many interviews, Pema Tseden's motivation for writing and making films is to show a Tibetan view of Tibet. He attempts to reclaim the representation of Tibet, which for so long has been a product of Chinese or Western imaginations, and to place it in Tibetan hands; to move away from mythologized, idealized, or propagandistic representations of Tibet's past; and to provide a fresh view of Tibet's present. Although motivation and themes are similar in both his Tibetan and Chinese stories, there are some stylistic differences; while his Chinese-language short stories sound direct, colloquial, and sharp, his Tibetan-language stories have retained a more classical, lyrical style. His choice of language is, of course, determined by his audience. He writes in Tibetan language for Tibetans, and in Chinese language for Chinese audiences, as well as for those Tibetans who only read Chinese. Although he often translates his Tibetan-language work into Chinese, he himself acknowledges that some of his stories

ACKNOWLEDGMENTS

The editors would like to thank A. E. Clark, Lan Wu, and Carl Robertson for their editorial suggestions on the stories translated from Chinese. Our heartfelt thanks go also to Françoise Robin, Lauran Hartley, and Tenzin Norbu Nangsal for their editorial suggestions on the stories translated from Tibetan. We are very grateful to our editors at SUNY Press, Christopher Ahn and Aimee Harrison, for believing in this project wholeheartedly and for their guidance and editorial support. Finally, we would like to thank Pema Tseden himself for having inspired us to produce this anthology in the first place and for his patience in answering questions and providing additional information.

AUTHOR'S PREFACE

Our minds and bodies, surrounded by a myriad of worldly affairs, can hardly get a moment of peace. Aspiring to find quiet time may sometimes feel like an extravagant hope. For me, writing is a way to achieve such inner peace. This is especially true when I write fiction. It allows me to return to the past, face the present, and look forward to the future.

I was born in the Tibetan areas, but then left to go elsewhere. I have been nurtured by Tibetan, Chinese, Western, and other cultures. These experiences integrated into my life and my creations, deeply influencing who I have become and allowing my creative work to show its current force.

Sometimes I don't know what kind of person I am—how who I was and who I am are related or different, or who my future self will end up being. Often, in both my life and my creative work, I find myself in a bewildered and helpless state, to the point of not finding a sense of direction or an exit point. But when I enter an exceptionally creative writing mood, I seem to be able to break away from perplexity and passiveness. My body and mind slowly relax to follow that wonderful rhythm that allows me to enter into my inner world, into the inner worlds of the characters of my stories. In these moments I feel completely at ease.

This is also the time when I can see more clearly into myself—can see some of my inner passion, sincerity, fragility, pettiness. Many times I write fiction for no other reason than to enter this state in which I can see and know myself more deeply.

All the words you want to say can be found in the texts you write.

Translated from the Chinese by Patricia Schiaffini-Vedani.

Wu Yao, *The Mark of the White Conch*

ORGYAN'S TEETH

Orgyan was a friend of mine from primary school. All that is well known. Later on, Orgyan was identified as a reincarnate lama. All that is likewise well known.

These are not the main things. The main thing is that when Orgyan reached the age of twenty, he died. When I spoke to many people of Orgyan's death, they said it was not proper to speak of a reincarnate lama's death like that; rather, it was more appropriate to say, "passed into nirvana." However, the two of us, Orgyan and I, had been playmates when we were young and then were also classmates in the five years of primary school. If it is necessary to describe a friend of the same age getting lassoed and caught by the lord of death as "passed into nirvana," then it is hard for me to unravel what to actually say. But my father, and mother especially, said it was not right to speak in that way of his death. If I did, I would not be giving respect to a great, holy being more endowed with wisdom and merit than I.

After listening to my parents, I no longer wished to talk about his death like I had. I can certainly say, if asked, that Orgyan possessed greater merit than I. After he was recognized as a reincarnate lama, many people, because of his position, felt that they had to prostrate to him. One time, my father and mother said they would bring me to the monastery where he lived and force me to prostrate three times to him. I really did not want to prostrate to him. He, himself, in the midst of a gathering of

Translated from the Tibetan by Michael Monhart. Originally published in *Light Rain* (*Sbrang char*), no. 3 (2012).

people, said it was not necessary for me to do so. But my parents would not back down. Insistent, they said I must by all means prostrate three times. As I stood there not knowing what to do, they continued to berate me, saying, "Because you were a classmate of the reincarnate lama for five years, maybe you think that you are like him? Or you don't want all sentient beings seeing you prostrate to him? Why do you think you don't have to do it to him?" As they were adamant, I was not able to refuse them. Even if they had said more, many people were already lining up behind me to prostrate, and so I had no choice but to also prostrate three times to him. As I did so, he stared at me with a slight smile, while at the same time not showing any sign that it was not necessary for me to prostrate. At that moment, I was really unhappy. However, later on, I accepted the reality of the situation, and I felt more at ease, for the reason that having many people prostrate to him was proof that he had more merit than I.

Still, if one were to say he was more intelligent and knowledgeable than I, that wouldn't be something I could entirely go along with. As we were schoolmates from the first through the fifth grades, there was no one more familiar with him. I can say, from the perspective of being there, that not once from the first through fifth grades did he pass a mathematics exam or do his homework on his own. From the first grade on, all of his mathematics work was work of mine that I let him have. If I put it in this way, it is perhaps hard for you to hear. Indeed it would be the case that if others were to explain it like this to me, I myself wouldn't believe it. But that is the fact. I can say with the Three Jewels of Buddhism as my witness and can even take an oath that it is so. Each time, after the teacher would give out the mathematics homework, his sole task was only to stand by waiting for me to finish writing out the assignment. That was it. If I did not finish writing out the homework, then he would not wander off to play outside with the other kids. At that time, I didn't think to blame him at all. If, for instance, he had gone to play with the others, I wouldn't have been anxious about the homework and wouldn't have faced up to doing it then. Thinking about it now, I think both of us clearly understood the situation. That is, if I didn't finish the homework, then he obviously knew that he too would not be able to finish it. When he copied my work, he was more meticulous than I. As soon as I had completed the homework, I would toss the writing book in front of Orgyan and run outside to play with the other classmates. Once, the teacher praised him, saying that his homework was very carefully done, which made me a bit unhappy.

But there was nothing I could do for him, as a friend, when taking the midterm or final exams. If someone was caught spying on another's exam paper, then both students' exams were torn up and each score marked a zero. Therefore, when we took our exams in the classroom, no one was able to get someone to cheat for them. Orgyan and I were also like that, we didn't cheat. Our math teacher was a woman in her thirties. We heard that she had separated from her husband and now lived alone. Later, we understood from what we heard others say that she had had a child, but that the child had died from a severe disease. Behind her back, the school's teachers said that was why her temperament was like it was. In any case, throughout primary school, Orgyan could not pass even one of his exams in mathematics.

All this was what we did when we were young.

I continued on through middle school and high school. In our area, the only middle school was in the main town of the district, and so it was necessary for me to go there. After graduating from high school, I found a job in a small town and the days passed by. However, after primary school, Orgyan was not able to continue on in school. As he was an only child, his parents said it was okay for him to stay at home. He himself did not want to continue going to school.

Once, during the summer retreat, I asked him why he didn't continue in school. At first he said it was his parents' wish that he do so, and I pretended that was true. Later, he asked if I wanted to know the real reason he didn't go back to school. When I said I did want to know, he replied that he was afraid of mathematics. I laughed a bit and said, "You could have copied my homework." He said that from the first grade on, each time he would take and copy the mathematics homework, he felt like he was making a mistake. Hearing him say this, I thought he was a pure man.

When I graduated from high school, we had both turned eighteen. As I explained before, I left our small town to go look for work, without thinking of him any longer, and he was recognized as a reincarnate lama. The next summer, when I came back home, he invited me to come to his monastery, which was very close to our hometown. After he had been recognized as a reincarnate lama, we had met just once, on the day that he was enthroned at his monastery. In our area, as a reincarnate lama, he had the highest status of anyone. Many of his followers from the surrounding area were part of his monastic community. On the day he was enthroned, a large number of devotees gathered to meet with him. Everyone brought offering scarves and other such offerings, and were prostrating to him with immeasurable respect. Was it not at that time that my parents compelled me also to prostrate to him?

This time when I went to see him, I took to his monastery offering scarves and other sorts of gifts. A monk led me to his room. He was sitting in the cross-legged meditation posture surrounded by Buddhist texts, rosaries, and other such religious items. After sending away the monk who had led me there, he looked at me, smiling. I felt at that moment, however, that there was automatically a sense of distance between us. After respectfully giving him a ceremonial offering scarf, I didn't think it necessary to prostrate to him. He motioned to me with his hand to come squat next to him. I saw then an expression on his face that was like when he was young, and seeing it, I felt that the distance between us was gone. Smiling, he said to me, "Last time, your parents made it hard for you by making you prostrate."

Though it was necessary to reply, I didn't really know how, but I did finally say, "Doesn't everyone have to prostrate to you? So it was okay for me also to do so."

Looking steadily at me, he said, "Now, as there is no one else here but us two, you don't need to have any worries about that."

Even though he spoke in that way, I still wasn't able to relax very much, so I gave him yet another ceremonial scarf.

He then asked me, "You were good at mathematics, like an expert. Why didn't you go to the university?"

There were many reasons I didn't go to the university, and as I had no desire to clearly spell them out for him, I found some excuses to give.

"I understand all that," he said. "Still, it is too bad."

Gradually, I began to relax. It felt like when the two of us were together when we were young. Likewise, he said, "Now you look like when we were young."

Because now it felt like there was no distance between us, I playfully asked him, "Are you still afraid of mathematics?"

Smiling and shaking his head back and forth, he said, "Remembering that, it still gives me a headache."

I replied, "Now, are you happy because no one at all can force you to do any work that you don't want to do?"

He replied, "Even though I'm a reincarnate lama, how could I just sit around doing nothing? These days, my teacher is teaching me astrology. And while even that has a connection to numbers, it is still easier than the mathematics we did when we were young."

Growing amazed, I said, "From all that I have heard, astrology is very complicated, several times more difficult than our primary school mathematics."

He replied, modestly, "I don't have a great understanding of it."

Again looking at him closely, I asked, "After you were recognized as a reincarnate lama, didn't your intelligence burst forth?"

Smiling as before, he said, "Nevertheless it became a habit at that time to rely upon you for the answer."

I continued to stare intently at him.

He then asked me, "I've heard that some expert has proved that adding one plus one can make three. How can that be true?"

I said to him, "This is an exceedingly deep mathematical problem. A few very skilled mathematicians have only now been able to prove it. From primary school through middle school, the fruits of my study were very good, but this problem I am completely unable to answer."

He went on to say, "I don't know any more besides that one and one makes two, two and two makes four, three and three makes six, four and four makes eight, five and five makes ten, six and six makes twelve, seven and seven makes fourteen, eight and eight makes sixteen, nine and nine makes eighteen, and ten and ten makes twenty."

I thought he would continue on in the same manner up to one hundred and one hundred makes two hundred, but he stopped at adding ten to ten to get twenty. I relaxed and breathed out a sigh, wondering how he had been able to learn astrology. But I only said, "really fast."

As if not hearing me, he said, "Even so, I cannot understand how one and one can make three."

Orgyan separated from the world of humans when he was twenty years old. I, however, have lived in the world of humans past the age of twenty. I know it is not proper to say of Orgyan that he died, separating from the world of humans, but I can't inwardly accustom myself to say of a friend of the same age that he "passed away into nirvana."

Still, this is not the main point. The main point is that now our ways have parted forever.

The very last time that Orgyan and I met was on New Year's Day in the year of his death. We both had reached twenty years old as the New Year celebrations began that year. I had found work in the town, but since then, no such luck had come in anything else that I did. In the past, I heard that people from our village and other villages, whenever starting something important, would go to where Orgyan lived and ask for assistance, and that afterwards, they would have good fortune in all their activities. I didn't have any faith in things like that, but in those years, I had met difficulties in just about everything from all directions and so, since it was the New Year, thought I could go to him and ask for help.

After Orgyan had been recognized as a reincarnate lama, the people in the village said that there had been many marvelous signs at the time of his birth. Some said flowers blossomed on fruit trees in the middle of winter. Others said that though there were not even clouds as small as a bird's head in the sky, the roar of thunder could be heard. Still others said a five-colored-rainbow encircled the sun. There was much talk then of many wonders. I had no belief in wonders like these; still it wasn't that I absolutely did not believe. As it was known that Orgyan and I had been friends in primary school, I was asked what especially distinguished qualities he had. In regard to that question, other than remembering that he had never done well on mathematics exams, I couldn't think of anything else.

Once, I did suddenly remember something that Orgyan had done when he was young. Through the meaning of that act, one was able to know that Orgyan, even as a young child, at least had an enlightened heart. This is what happened when we were in third grade:

One day we were playing on the banks of the Machu river. On the banks of the Machu there was a strange, unusually large boulder, and Orgyan liked to go there regularly to play. According to legend, once when Padmasambhava was going along the Machu, after coming to that place as it was nearing darkness, he, along with his older and younger wives, rested with their backs against the rock for the night. It was said that at daybreak, the shape of his back was visible, imprinted in the face of the boulder with the impression of his older wife on one side, that of his younger on the other. Usually there were many religious pilgrims who visited that place. Also, there were many Nyingma monasteries there because of this legend (as Padmasambhava is said to be the founder of that sect).

That day though, there was not even a single pilgrim around. After wandering around, playing for about half a day, we started to return home. On the way, as we were going along the sandy bank of the river, we saw a fish wriggling in the sand. As soon as I saw the fish, I said, without thinking much, "That is a big fish! We can sell it to the Chinese there doing road work. They will eat it."

Orgyan, paying me no attention, ran over to the fish in the sand and, after taking hold of it, said, "No, it's not right to act like that. I will put it back into the water."

Seeing him gently take the still wriggling fish into the palm of his hand, I said, "Put it down, put it down now! From here to the Machu is a long way. The fish will die before you get there."

Orgyan said to me, "You go back home. I'm for sure going to put this fish back in the water." After which, grasping the fish, he ran off in the direction of the Machu. I watched his back as he ran and, after waiting for a moment, ran after him.

On the way, seeing that the fish didn't quiver at all, I said, "Throw it away. It really is dead." But Orgyan kept running in the direction of the Machu, ignoring me.

When we arrived at the Machu river, we were both panting, gasping for breath.

Orgyan gently put the fish in the water. At first, it just floated on the surface, not moving at all. Orgyan and I stayed there, staring at it, also holding our breaths. Then the fish quivered, then once more. And then, in a flash, it quickly entered the depths of the river.

When I would talk about this event, people said that there were certainly many distinctive qualities that made a great person like him different from ordinary people.

About Orgyan, there was various talk about unusual things, and that, along with my memories of the time when he was young and the many small things that he did, gradually made him appear to me as having especially distinguished good qualities that were really different from others. Because of all that, on the first day of that New Year, I prepared some gifts and a long, spotless offering scarf and went to meet with him.

As before, Orgyan treated me like a close friend; however, unlike before, I felt a spontaneous sense of faith in him arise within me.

After respectfully presenting the offering scarf and gifts to him, I stepped back and was just about to prostrate to him.

Laughing, Orgyan said, "Between the two of us, it's not necessary to do that." After which, he gestured with his hand, saying, "Sit here next to me."

I, however, prostrated to him three times.

He sat cross-legged, looking at me.

I stammered out, "Orgyan, Orgyan, Rinpoche, because all my work this past year has not gone well in any way, this year by all means please give me some assistance."

Orgyan, smiling, asked me, "Do you have trust?"

Respectfully, I replied, "Everyone says that you have blessings."

The smile on Orgyan's face widened more than before and he said, "My very good friend, certainly I will fully grant your request for help."

After he said this, he closed his eyes, chanted many prayers, gave me a spoonful of water from the altar to drink, and finally bestowed upon me a protective cord that he had blessed, and said, "Always wear this protective cord."

I thanked him over and over from the depths of my heart, but again he said, "Between the two of us that is not necessary."

Then, as if suddenly recalling something, he said, "Last month, I met someone."

"Who?" I asked.

"If you think a moment, you'll know who."

My head spinning, I said, "I don't know."

Still smiling, he said, "Think about it a little more! It is someone to whom we both have a connection."

But after thinking more about it, my head was still spinning.

Finally, he said, "Our mathematics teacher from when we were young came here."

Now, getting what he was saying, I really was surprised, as I had not seen her at all since finishing school.

He went on, "She came and asked for my help."

"Was it her?" I questioned.

"It was. It really was her. She had married and given birth to a child," he answered.

"Did she talk about when were young?" I asked.

He said, "She didn't. When I talked to her about when we were young, and that the results of my mathematics studies were very poor, she didn't want to talk about it. I said I accumulated many faults."

I did not believe that was the case.

He went on, "She prostrated to me three times and fervently requested help for her child."

"And then?" I asked.

He replied, "I promised to always help her, and she said thank you to me as she left."

I said, "That really is inconceivable."

"She hadn't changed much, a bit more peaceful than before," he said.

I said, "When we were young, she certainly faced many difficulties in her life."

He said, "Do you know what question I asked her?"

"I don't know."

"I asked her the reason why if you add one plus one, you get three."

"What did she say?" I asked.

"She said she was only a primary school math teacher, so she couldn't comprehend the profound theory of something like that."

I again recalled the time before when he had asked me about this question.

He continued on, "In the future, I want to clearly know the reason why if you add one plus one you get three."

After that New Year, I heard that Orgyan had forever parted ways with the world of human beings. Now, even though I am able to call Orgyan's separating from this world of humans as "passing into nirvana," still, that is not the main point. The main thing is that after Orgyan passed away, the monastery and the faithful around the monastery made preparations to construct a memorial stupa to him and, after intensive discussion, said that Orgyan's teeth were to be placed inside as an offering. However, the important point isn't the construction of the stupa. It is not unusual to construct a memorial stupa for a reincarnate lama who has obtained a high status.

The important point is that they prepared to insert fifty-eight of Orgyan's teeth into the memorial stupa.

In the usual person, how can there be fifty-eight teeth? Even for an unusual person, it's not possible for there to be fifty-eight teeth.

But to speak truthfully, before this, I also didn't know how many teeth a person usually has. Therefore I asked an elderly person, "How many teeth does a person usually have?"

The elderly person thought it over and said, "Most have thirty teeth."

But they couldn't be certain about their answer, so I again asked another elderly person, "How many teeth does a person usually have?"

That elderly person answered without having to think about it at all. "Thirty-two."

As that elderly person looked quite sure of his answer, I wanted to take that number as the right one.

But to decide conclusively if that was the right number or not, I went to an internet café.

The supervisor of the internet café said, "You must put your name in the register."

I said, "Why?"

"It's the rule of the higher authorities," he replied.

"I have something I am looking for. It won't take more than a few minutes. If I don't sign the register is that okay?"

"You have to sign it. It's the rule of the higher authorities."

I said, "You are really being irritating about this."

He replied angrily, "I'm just a worker here. I'm only making four or five hundred yuan each month. Why are you talking to me like this?"

Having no choice, I gave my name to him for the register.

While writing my name and so forth at the top of a page in an old notebook, he said, "You look, here is the register of all who have come in here. This is the rule of the higher authorities. I don't have any choice."

I stood there, paying no attention to him.

After filling out the register, he asked me, "What are you looking for?"

"I'm looking for how many teeth a person usually has."

While grinning at me, he said, "You don't know even that?"

Angered, I said, "Well, you tell me! How many teeth does a person usually have?"

After thinking about it, he scratched his head, saying, "Strangely enough, if I had to say how many teeth a person usually has, I don't really know. How many? Maybe more than twenty?"

I laughed and said, "Next time, you should count precisely!"

Then I went to go online on the computer. On the way, I turned back, and as I looked, I saw he had put his finger in his mouth and was carefully counting the teeth in his mouth.

I typed into the Google search bar, "How many teeth does a person usually have?" and immediately more than one hundred results appeared.

I opened up one result that had many replies to it.

Someone called "Beautiful Dentist from Peking" wrote only two digits, the number "28."

Another called "Winter's Cuckoo Bird" had answered like this, "28+4 as some people are not born with the innermost teeth, the wisdom teeth."

Someone else called "Even if One Will Die Tomorrow, Learn!" wrote, "A person with a full set of teeth has 32, but as some do not have wisdom teeth the number can be 28–32."

Still more, someone called "I am King" had written in inordinate detail. Looking at it, I was taken aback. Up to now I had had never known that even teeth had so many qualities and that it was not possible to know, once and for all, how many there could be.

After thinking about this, the opinion that came naturally was that one should, in the future, take good care of one's teeth.

But all of that aside, the monastery was able to clearly know that all of the fifty-eight teeth found to give as offerings in the stupa were not all Orgyan's teeth, that some were other people's teeth.

The manager of the monastery had no choice but to go to Orgyan's father and mother with the teeth placed in an offering scarf for them to identify which were not their son's teeth. However, Orgyan's parents said they had previously finished giving the monastery Orgyan's teeth and all other things connected to him from when he was young, and now they said it was difficult to distinguish which were really their son's teeth and which were not.

When the stupa was near completion, the monastery's manager, having exhausted all means to figure out whose teeth were whose, put the fifty-eight teeth, religious texts, and so forth into the stupa as an offering.

Following the completion of the stupa, many religious pilgrims, and even I, got accustomed to going there regularly.

One time, when I was making a circumambulation of the stupa, I suddenly recalled something from when we were young.

One day, after being let out of class, Orgyan said to me that we'd do the homework after going to his house. When we arrived at his house, I began to do the mathematics homework, and he waited next to me. After I had finished writing out the homework, I handed it over to him, and he meticulously copied it.

At that moment, one of my front teeth suddenly started hurting, and as I could not bear the pain, I cried out.

Orgyan went to get his father, and they came back together. His father, after looking at my pained tooth for a moment, said, "The tooth has to be pulled out."

I was extremely frightened at having my tooth pulled, and even though I did whatever I could to avoid him, he chased after me with a thread. After wrapping the thread around my hurting tooth, he gestured to me in an up and down direction.

I felt a sharp pain inside my mouth, and then that tooth was in his father's hand.

Smiling, he gave me the tooth and said, "Wrap it in wool and throw it out the window to the roof!"

After wrapping the tooth in wool and bending my head upwards, I worried that I could not throw the tooth out the window and up onto the roof.

Orgyan's father, smiling, said, "Do you know what should be said when you throw the tooth away?"

Nodding my head, I said, "Sure, I know."

Bending my head upwards, looking out the window, I recited, "I abandon my bad tooth, like a pig tooth. In return, may I have a perfect white tooth like a white conch." After reciting this again, I tossed the tooth wrapped in wool out the window and up on the roof.

Orgyan's father said, "That's right, now you'll surely grow a good tooth," and I was happy.

Arriving at this juncture in my story, I also remember something else. Soon after Orgyan had been recognized as a reincarnate lama, some monks came to Orgyan's house and said to his father and mother that, among various things of Orgyan's that they had taken, a few teeth were still missing. Not taking any time, they went to the roof of the house, searched again, and found some of Orgyan's teeth from when he was young, wrapped each of them carefully in an offering scarf as if they were pearls, and carried them away. It was in this way I think, that the tooth of mine, which I had thrown out the window and on to the roof, was also carried away by the monks and is now among those things put inside the majestic stupa and held as objects of faith by all the devout.

THARLO

Tharlo kept a small braid. The braid swung constantly back and forth behind his head very noticeably. Over time, everyone just called him "Little Braid" and forgot his name.

At the beginning of the year, the District Chief of Police came to the village to call all the villagers into one assembly and register everyone for identity cards. At one point in the procedure, after he had been shouting the name "Tharlo" for some time without an answer, he asked the Village Head, "Don't you have anyone in your village named 'Tharlo'?"

The Village Head thought for a moment and said, "It seems there is no such person in the village."

The Chief replied sternly, "You cannot say 'seems.' You must be positive that there is no such person in your village."

The Village Head pondered a long while but still could not recall anyone with the name. He said, "We have several hundred people in our village these days, and I cannot recall precisely."

The Chief eyed him, "Then how can you serve as the Village Head!?"

The Head replied warmly, "Just because I'm Village Head doesn't make me remember everyone's name. My duty is to lead the entire village from poverty to prosperity. And then—what with all of the women and girls giving birth one after the other without any concern about fines or whatever—just in the past two days there were five more!—you tell me

Translated from the Chinese by Carl Robertson. Originally published in *Qinghai River* (*Qinghai hu*), no. 11 (2012).

how I should be able to recall so many names. Many of them don't even have names yet!"

The Chief laughed, "As the Village Head you ought to remember the names of the people in the village."

The Village Head glared, "Then can you remember all the people registered in your District?"

The Chief said, "This is different, you are the head of the village."

The Head said, "Well, you are the chief of the district."

The Chief laughed. "Since you don't know about him, I'll just cross out his name, but when he is not able to stay in a hotel in the city, don't blame me for it."

The Head also laughed and waved the Auditor over and asked, "Is there someone named Tharlo in our village?"

The middle-aged Auditor thought for some time but still could not recall anyone of that name.

He saw that the Head and Chief were waiting for him to answer, so he called over the head of one of the local community areas.

He said to the Community Head, "Do you know if there is anyone in our village named Tharlo?"

The Community Head thought for some time and then suddenly laughed. "Ah yes, why not? It is Little Braid!"

The Village Head and the Auditor both laughed. "Yes, yes! It is Little Braid! Tharlo is Little Braid and Little Braid is Tharlo, they are one and the same. Look how we nearly forgot his name!"

The Chief looked at them suspiciously.

The Village Head quickly explained, "Little Braid is Tharlo's nickname. We are so used to using his nickname, we've forgotten his real name, so that's what this is all about."

The Chief asked, "And what about him?"

The Head said, "Oh, well, it's like this: he's an orphan with no one to look after him. For many years, he's taken on the sheep of a number of families and has gone alone to herd them in the mountains. We don't know who gave him his nickname. We've called him that since he was in his teens."

The Chief said, "To process an identity card we need a photograph of the subject. You must find a way to bring him in."

The Head said, "For a photo today?"

The Chief said, "The photos can't be done today. He must go to the District's designated location to get his photo taken."

The Head said, "Then in two days' time I'll manage to get him down from the mountains and go to the District."

After about ten days or so, Tharlo finally arrived at the rural district police station.

The District Chief glanced at the braid tied with red at the back of his head and asked, "You must be Little Braid?"

Tharlo was a little taken aback. Looking at the District Chief, he asked, "How did you know?"

The District Chief laughed. "We are police officers, so we certainly know more than others do."

Tharlo spoke respectfully, "No wonder that you caught some of the bad people."

The Chief said with a small laugh, "Do you mean that there are some bad people that we haven't caught?"

Tharlo said, "Oh yes. The year before last, three of my ewes and nine of my lambs were stolen. You police were not able to catch the thieves."

The Chief said, "Did you report it?"

Tharlo said, "Of course I reported it. I reported it to the Village Head."

The Chief said, "The Village Head is very busy, maybe he forgot about it."

Tharlo said, "Maybe. But the Village Head afterwards swore that he reported it to you here."

The Chief said, "The loss of several sheep—there are just too many cases like that."

Tharlo said, "But last year, thieves stole twelve sheep and were caught by you after a month and a half! You are amazing anyway."

The Chief laughed, "*Ha ha.* If there are too many sheep stolen then we have to take care of that!"

With an expression of deference, Tharlo said, "You still found them after they'd been stolen for over a month, you are really outstanding!"

The Chief laughed again, "*Ha ha.*" Watching Tharlo's deferential attitude, he assumed a humble tone and said, "It's as it should be, just to serve the people!"

Tharlo laughed with him and said, "I know that expression. Chairman Mao said it. I learned it in school when I was little."

The Chief could not help but look Tharlo over. "You went to school?"

Tharlo earnestly said, "I did, how could I not have? I went to grade school. My grades were pretty good too. I even memorized the essay, 'Serve the People.'"

The Chief said, "Is that so? Can you still remember it?"

Tharlo said, "Of course I do. I can completely recall anything I've memorized. I don't ever forget."

The Chief said, "Then recite it, and let's see."

Tharlo thought for a moment, then he began rattling it off:

"'Serve the People,' September 8, 1944. Mao Zedong.

"Our Communist Party and the Eighth Route and New Fourth Armies led by our Party are battalions of the revolution. These battalions of ours are wholly dedicated to the liberation of the people and work entirely in the people's interests. Comrade Zhang Side was in the ranks of these battalions.

"All men must die, but death can vary in its significance. The ancient Chinese writer Sima Qian said, 'Though death befalls all men alike, it may be weightier than Mount Tai or lighter than a feather.' To die for the people is weightier than Mount Tai but to work for the Fascists and die for the exploiters and oppressors is lighter than a feather. Comrade Zhang Side died for the people and his death is indeed weightier than Mount Tai.

"If we have shortcomings, we are not afraid to have them pointed out and criticized, because we serve the people. Anyone, no matter who, may point

out our shortcomings. If he is right, we will correct them. If what he propos-
es will benefit the people, we will act upon it. The idea of 'better troops and
simpler administration' was put forward by Mr. Li Dingming, who is not a
Communist. He made a good suggestion, which is of benefit to the people, and
we adopted it. If, in the interests of the people, we persist in doing what is right
and correct what is wrong, our ranks will surely thrive. '

"*We hail from all corners of the country and have joined together for a*
common revolutionary objective. And we need the vast majority of the peo-
ple with us on the road to this objective. Today, we already lead base areas
with a population of ninety one million, but this is not enough to liberate the
whole nation. More are needed. In times of difficulty we must not lose sight
of our achievements. We must see the bright future and must pluck up our
courage. The Chinese people are suffering; it is our duty to save them and
we must exert ourselves in the struggle. Wherever there is struggle, there is
sacrifice, and death is a common occurrence. But we have the interests of the
people and the sufferings of the great majority at heart, and when we die for
the people it is a worthy death. Nevertheless, we should do our best to avoid
unnecessary sacrifices. Our cadres must show concern for every soldier, and
all people in the revolutionary ranks must care for one another, must love and
help each another.

"*From now on, when anyone in our ranks who has done useful work*
dies, be he soldier or cook, we should hold a funeral ceremony and a memorial
meeting in his honor. This should become the rule. And it should be introduced
among the people as well. When someone dies in a village, let a memorial
meeting be held. In this way, we express our mourning for the dead and unite
all the people."

When Tharlo finished the last breath of his recitation, he saw that the
Chief was looking at him with his mouth wide open.

Tharlo said, "How was it? Did I get it right?"

The Chief recovered his usual expression. He said, "I had no idea
you were a genius!"

Tharlo said with some awkwardness, "It's just that my memory is a little better than others."

The Chief asked, "When did you memorize this lesson?"

Tharlo said, "At fourteen, in grade school. At that time, our school lessons were basically the words of Chairman Mao. I can still recite many of his sayings."

The Chief said, "You are really amazing. How old are you now?"

Tharlo said, "Twenty nine."

The Chief said in amazement, "*Ts ts*! If I had your memory I would have gone to university long ago!"

Tharlo said, "After grade school, I didn't continue. My parents died, and my relatives did not take me in. They said that since I have a good memory, I should herd sheep for some families in the village and keep good track of the color and kind of each one. They said that as long as I did not lose any, I'd be able to have enough to eat anyway. The only thing for me to do was to herd sheep in the mountains. When I began, I had one hundred and sixty sheep. The second year, they increased by sixty, the third year by forty seven, the fourth year by eleven. That was the year of the blizzards in which many sheep died—*ai!*—but still they have increased every year, and they've never decreased, and now the herd has increased to three hundred and seventy five, including two hundred and seven white, seventy three black, and ninety five spotted sheep, one hundred and thirty four with horns, two hundred and forty one without."

The Chief stared at him, gaping. After a while he finally said, "It's too bad, too bad. It is such a pity for you!"

Tharlo replied, "I feel that by helping others herd sheep, I am serving the people, even though they give me ten odd sheep every year and even pay me a little."

The Chief quickly nodded and said, "Yes, yes, oh yes, of course you are."

Tharlo said, "I like that expression from Chairman Mao, where he said, 'Certain it is that all die, but some deaths are as weighty as Mount Tai, others as light as a feather.'"

The Chief recovered himself and said, "Now although you've recited it all very well, do you think you may not have learned the lesson properly yet? This quotation was not from Chairman Mao; it was Sima Qian who said it. Sima Qian was a great literary writer."

Tharlo said, "Really? So what is the relationship between Chairman Mao and Sima Qian?"

The Chief laughed. "There is no relationship. Sima Qian lived in ancient times. Chairman Mao lived in modern times. They have no connection at all."

Somewhat confused, Tharlo asked, "Then what of this quotation, 'To die for the good of the people is weightier than Mount Tai, to die for Fascist traitors or die for those who exploit and oppress the people is lighter than a feather. Comrade Zhang Side died for the good of the people. His death is weightier than Mount Tai.' Is this quotation from Chairman Mao?"

The Chief said, "Yes, yes. If you die it will most definitely be like Comrade Zhang Side, weightier than Mount Tai, but you are still far from death. But I can still see that you are a good person, a person as good as Zhang Side."

Tharlo asked, "How can you see that I am as good a person as Zhang Side?"

The Chief said, "Whether someone is good or bad we are able to see it in a glance. We police officers have this particular ability."

Tharlo replied, "Please tell me how you really are able to see whether someone is good or bad."

With a mysterious smile, the Chief said, "Now that I really cannot tell you—we depend on this skill for our livelihood!"

Tharlo looked a little crestfallen, but in his eyes there was still a glimmer of admiration.

The Chief exclaimed again, "Your memory is remarkable!"

Tharlo seemed to suddenly remember something. "I came to get my photo taken. The Village Head had me come."

The Chief looked askance at him. "Why is it that you are only coming now? The photographers left long ago."

Tharlo said, "The Head did not send someone to replace me until yesterday. I hurried right over today."

The Chief said, "Then you'll have to go to the County City to get your photo taken."

Tharlo said, "Is it alright to not have a photo?"

The Chief said, "No, we have to process your identity card."

Tharlo asked, "What is an 'identity card'?"

The Chief said, "If you have an identity card, then when you go into some city, other people will know who you are. They will know where you come from."

Tharlo said, "Isn't it good enough that I know myself where I come from?"

Here the Chief seemed to remember something and asked, "What are you called?"

Tharlo answered, "Little Braid."

The Chief said, "I'm asking about your real name."

Tharlo thought for a moment and then answered, "Tharlo."

The Chief said, "Tharlo, *hmm*, yes. Go to the County City today and look up the De Ji Photo Studio. There is a woman in there named De Ji. Just tell her that the police station had you go get your photo taken, and she will know what to do."

Tharlo laughed a little. "It seems that my real name is not my own name. When I hear it, it seems a little strange."

The Chief looked at the digital watch on his wrist. "You'd better stop talking and get a move on. You may still catch the bus to the County."

Tharlo did ride the bus to the County City.

When he got down from the bus onto the street, he felt a little dazed. He saw people coming and going, running left and right. He had no idea which direction he should go.

He saw a grade school student wearing a red kerchief coming towards him and quickly asked, "Hi little friend, do you know where the De Ji Photo Studio is?"

The child took a look at him, saw the braid behind his head and energetically shook his head.

Tharlo said, "Don't be afraid, little friend. I'm called Little Braid. I need to go to the De Ji Photo Studio to get my photo taken."

The young student said happily, "If you let me take a look at your braid, I'll take you there."

Tharlo gladly squatted down to let him look at it.

The young student, examining the braid with profound concentration, said, "Our teacher said that people only wore braids during the Qing Dynasty. Why do you keep a braid?"

Tharlo looked at the young student. "Don't go thinking that I am from the Qing Dynasty!"

The young student said, "I'll have to ask my teacher about it."

Tharlo stood up and said, "Please take me to the photo studio."

The young student mumbled haltingly, "I can't remember exactly where it is."

Tharlo looked worried. He suddenly pulled out a ten kuai bill and said, "If you take me there I'll give you ten kuai."

Shortly afterwards the student had taken him to the door of the De Ji Photo Studio, had taken the ten kuai bill from Tharlo, and had flown directly into a small shop opposite.

When Tharlo opened the door, he saw a woman taking a man's photo. Several people were seated to the side. As soon as the man made a forced, fake smile, the camera flashed—*punang paneh!* The man then stood to one side, and another man sat on the stool and leaned forward.

Tharlo entered. The woman did not greet him but kept right on with her business.

Tharlo stood in the doorway and said, "Is this the De Ji Photo Studio?"

The woman looked over. "Yes it's the De Ji Photo Studio. Can I help you?"

Tharlo said, "I am looking for De Ji."

The woman stopped and looked suspiciously at Tharlo. "I am De Ji."

A smile crossed Tharlo's face, "I am here to have my photo taken. The Police Station had me come here."

De Ji said, "For an 'enlarged portrait' photo?"

Tharlo said, "I don't know. He said it's for some card."

De Ji laughed and said, "*Ha*! You should have said so! You need an enlarged portrait shot to process your identity card. All that nonsense—I thought there was something else going on. Have a seat for a bit. They are all getting their photos taken too."

The others looked at Tharlo and laughed. Tharlo sat beside them.

After the others had left, De Ji waved Tharlo over. "Now we'll take yours."

Tharlo went over and sat on the stool in front of the white studio background.

De Ji picked up a camera and walked over. She suddenly noticed that Tharlo had a small braid behind his head and asked, "Why are you growing a braid?"

Tharlo said, "I've had it since I was little."

De Ji said, "It may not be acceptable to take a portrait shot this way."

Tharlo said, "Why not?"

De Ji said, "At the police station they won't be able to tell if you're male or female."

Tharlo replied earnestly, "I just came from the station. The Chief never said anything about it."

De Ji said, laughing, "Alright, alright, I'll take your picture and let it be."

Tharlo sat straight up like the previous subjects and prepared to put a smile on his face.

De Ji made several motions while holding the camera then walked over and touched Tharlo's tousled hair. She said, "I think you ought to wash your hair. Your hair is too messy right now. It won't look good if I take your photo like this."

Tharlo said, "Let it be messy. Go ahead and take it. I'm not that particular about it."

De Ji said resolutely, "Once your identity card is done you'll just have to use it the rest of your life. Is there anything wrong with having a good picture taken for it?"

Tharlo looked at De Ji without speaking.

De Ji pointed out the window at a hair salon facing across the street and said, "Go and get a quick shampoo over there. It's run by a good friend of mine."

Tharlo stood up impatiently and walked out of the photo studio.

As Tharlo walked into the hair salon, a girl with short hair stood and greeted him.

Tharlo looked at the girl with renewed interest, "Are you the friend of De Ji who works in the photo studio opposite? I'm here to have my hair washed."

The girl with short hair scrutinized him carefully then had him sit in a chair, after which she went behind him and spoke to him from the mirror. "It is five kuai for a wet shampoo, ten kuai for a dry shampoo. Do you want dry or wet?"

Tharlo looked at the face of the girl in the mirror. He said, "What is a 'dry shampoo'?"

The girl with short hair laughed lightly. She said, "A shampoo without water."

Tharlo continued, "How do you shampoo without water?"

The short-haired girl said, "Well, it's very pleasant anyway—if you get it you'll know what I mean."

Tharlo said, "Dry shampoo then."

The short-haired girl squeezed out shampoo on the top of Tharlo's head and lightly massaged his hair.

Tharlo continued to watch the short-haired girl in the mirror before him.

The short-haired girl looked back at him in the mirror and asked, "Is it pleasant?"

Tharlo said, "It really is very pleasant."

As if to make small talk, the short-haired girl said, "You haven't had your hair washed for quite some time, have you?"

Tharlo said, "I am a shepherd. There is not much water for washing hair."

The short-haired girl acted surprised. She said, "Oh, is that so? You must have a lot of sheep then?"

Tharlo said earnestly, "Altogether I have three hundred and seventy five sheep, including one hundred and thirty three rams, one hundred and sixty eight ewes, and seventy four half-grown lambs. Among those one hundred and sixty eight ewes, this year one hundred and twenty four are still able to bear lambs. Forty four of them are already too old to become pregnant."

The short-haired girl stopped kneading his hair and looked at Tharlo's face in the mirror with a touch of surprise. "You have a good memory!"

Tharlo said bashfully, "You have to remember the condition of each of your sheep to take good care of them."

The short-haired girl began gently massaging his hair again. Looking at Tharlo in the mirror she asked, "Then how much money are all these sheep worth?"

Tharlo said, "Today I sold off two rams. They brought six hundred kuai. Currently one ewe is about two hundred kuai. If it's a pregnant ewe, it could go higher, to about two hundred and fifty or so. A lamb is over one hundred each, so altogether they're worth about eighty to ninety thousand kuai."

The short-haired girl gaped and said, "That much!?"

Tharlo said, "But not all three hundred and seventy five sheep belong to me! I only have something over one hundred."

The short-haired girl said, "Still that's a lot."

She then had Tharlo rinse his hair. Tharlo went over and sat below a water faucet.

While he rinsed his hair, Tharlo asked, "Isn't this a dry shampoo? Why use water to shampoo?"

The short-haired girl laughed. "Even though it's a dry shampoo, you still have to rinse the shampoo out of the hair to get it clean."

Tharlo did not say anything.

When his hair was rinsed, the short-haired girl had Tharlo go back to the stool in front of the mirror, turned on a blow dryer and dried out his hair.

Tharlo returned to staring at the girl in the mirror.

The short-haired girl laughed while drying his hair. "Why do you keep staring at me—am I that pretty?"

Tharlo did not look away. "When I first came in I would have thought you were a boy, if it weren't for your earrings."

The short-haired girl laughed. "Short hair is popular in the city. It's a trendy style."

Tharlo said, "But you are a Tibetan girl. How can a Tibetan girl cut her hair so short?"

The short-haired girl laughed again. "I cut my hair short to wait for a long-haired fellow like you to meet up with me!"

Now Tharlo did not know what to say. He lowered his gaze from the short-haired girl's face and looked in some other direction.

The short-haired girl finished drying Tharlo's hair, placed her hand on Tharlo's shoulder, and examined Tharlo's face in the mirror. Tenderly she said, "Now that you're cleaned up a bit, you're very handsome."

Tharlo felt awkward. He quickly pulled a fifty-kuai bill from his pocket and gave it to the girl. "Here's your fee."

The short-haired girl took the money. "Do you have any change? I can't make change for this."

Tharlo said, "If you don't have change then just keep it."

Before the short-haired girl could say anything, Tharlo had already run out of the hair salon.

When Tharlo arrived at the entrance to the photo studio, he saw that there were already several people inside, so he remained outside and began to smoke.

As he smoked, Tharlo's gaze wandered over to the hair studio across the street. He saw that the short-haired girl inside was just then looking out the glass window towards him. He smoked while watching the short-haired girl behind the window. The short-haired girl looked towards him and laughed.

Just then, several young people who seemed to be college students came walking down the street. One of them came towards him and struck up a conversation. "We are college students from the interior [of China]. We're traveling through but we think you look very different. Are you an artist?"

Tharlo continued smoking while looking at them with curiosity, as if he didn't understand what they had said. His face bore a very serious expression.

Another one said, "Look at the expression in his eyes, so penetrating. He is most definitely an artist of some depth."

Tharlo ignored them. After he had finished smoking his cigarette, had thrown the butt on the ground and energetically ground it out, he said, "Actually I am a shepherd."

Still another said, "Listen to him! How deeply he speaks. He is definitely an artist."

Just then, seeing several people emerge from the photo studio, he went in.

When De Ji saw him she said, "Just see how different you look with your hair cleaned up a little. You really are quite handsome!"

Tharlo was uncomfortable with the praise. He walked directly over and sat on the stool in front of the white cloth.

De Ji walked over while working with the camera. "Do you want a quick photo or a slow photo?"

Tharlo did not understand. "What is a 'quick photo' and a 'slow photo?'"

De Ji said, "You can pick up a quick photo today, but you will need to wait until tomorrow for the slow one."

Tharlo said, "Then I want the quick photo."

De Ji said, "A quick photo is twenty kuai, a slow one is ten."

Tharlo said, "That's alright, give me the quick one."

De Ji faced him and pressed the shutter release.

De Ji walked behind a counter and faced Tharlo, who was still sitting on the stool, and said, "Come pay the fee."

Tharlo went over to pay her. Tharlo again took out a fifty-kuai bill and handed it to De Ji. "Can you make change?"

De Ji took a look at the bill he'd handed her, said, "Yes," and began rummaging for change in the drawer. As she sorted through the bills, she asked Tharlo, "Just now I saw you outside talking to several young people—what did they say to you?"

Tharlo said, "They asked me if I'm an artist."

De Ji looked at him closely for a moment. She laughed. "Really?"

Tharlo said, "Yes. That is what they asked me."

De Ji laughed. "And what did you say?"

Tharlo said, "I said I herd sheep."

De Ji laughed right out loud.

Tharlo said, "What is an 'artist'?"

De Ji laughed. "An artist is someone who wears a small braid like you and grows long hair."

Tharlo looked at De Ji as if he didn't quite understand. Just then, De Ji found the change. She handed a handful to Tharlo and said, "Come get your photo in half an hour."

Tharlo stood on the street outside the photo studio once more, smoking. The short-haired girl came out from the hair salon and walked up to him.

"You're smoking?"

Tharlo said, "*Hm*, yes, smoking."

The short-haired girl said, "I saw you just now through the window —I think you are really handsome."

Again Tharlo didn't know how to act. As he finished one cigarette he began smoking a second.

The short-haired girl said, "Let's go to a bar tonight."

Tharlo said, "I've never been to a bar."

The short-haired girl said, "It will be fun. With you so handsome there will be plenty of girls interested in you."

Again Tharlo did not know what to do.

After half an hour had finally passed, Tharlo went to pick up the photo. As he took it out, he saw his own portrait and blurted out, "How ugly it came out!"

That night, Tharlo drank a large quantity of beer inside an extremely noisy bar. When he awoke in the morning he discovered the short-haired girl lying by his side.

Tharlo sat up nervously. The short-haired girl awoke too and laughed.

Tharlo could not look the short-haired girl in the eyes. The short-haired girl said, "Do you like me?"

Tharlo was suddenly very tense. He sat without moving.

The short-haired girl said, "Last night you said you like me."

The short-haired girl caressed Tharlo's small braid and said, "I like your braid."

Tharlo was as tense as ever.

The short-haired girl placed her head against Tharlo's shoulder. "Take me somewhere with you. I don't want to stay here."

As if finding a chance to speak for the first time, Tharlo said, "I've never been anywhere."

The short-haired girl said, "Then I'll take you. We can go to Lhasa, Beijing, Shanghai, Guangzhou, Hong Kong—we could go anywhere!"

Tharlo said, "I have never even thought of going to any of those places before."

The short-haired girl said, "If you were to choose, where would you want to go?"

Tharlo said, "I would go to Lhasa, of course."

The short-haired girl said, "Then we'll go to Lhasa."

Tharlo said, "I hear it costs a lot of money to go there. I don't have that much."

The short-haired girl said, "Sell your sheep off, then you'll have money, won't you?"

Tharlo said, "The sheep are not all mine, some of them belong to others."

At noon, Tharlo arrived at the police station. When the Chief saw him, he said, "You take a trip to the County and you become quite handsome indeed!"

Tharlo said, "I may have met a bad person on this trip."

The Chief was surprised. "You must immediately report any bad persons to us as soon as you encounter them."

Tharlo replied, "Right now I can't tell for sure yet whether or not they are a bad person."

The Chief laughed. "Ah you, Little Braid. You must have evidence to report a bad person or else you will have to face the consequences of the Law."

Judging from his expression, Tharlo seemed to have something caught in his throat. He said nothing.

The Chief said, "What about your photo?"

Tharlo quickly took out the photo and handed it to the Chief, adding "It came out quite ugly."

The Chief said, "That's the enlarged portrait format—it has to be done like that."

Tharlo said nothing more.

The Chief collected the photo, and after recording it, he said, "Alright—come back in a month to pick up your registration."

Tharlo was about to walk out when the Chief stopped him. "Let me ask you a personal question—why did you decide to grow a little braid?"

Tharlo sat back down. "This. . . ."

The Chief asked eagerly, " 'This' what?"

Tharlo said, "Actually there was no particular reason."

With a note of disappointment, the Chief said, "If you don't want to say, it's no matter. You have your right."

Observing the Chief, Tharlo said, "It really wasn't anything, it's just that I saw a movie."

The Chief perked up. "Can you tell me about it?"

Tharlo said, "When I had graduated from grade school, but before I had gone into the mountains to herd sheep, I borrowed some money and traveled to the County City."

The Chief said, "And then?"

Tharlo said, "And then I went to see a movie."

The Chief said, "What does this have to do with you growing a braid?"

Tharlo said, "Because I did not grow the braid until I had seen the movie."

The Chief said, "But how did you get the idea?"

Tharlo said, "In the movie there was a man who had a small braid. There were a lot of women interested in him."

The Chief laughed aloud. He said, "Then after you grew your little braid were there a lot of women interested in you?"

Tharlo said, "None of the girls in the village like me. They all say I'm a stingy tightwad."

The Chief stopped laughing. "What movie was this that you saw?"

Tharlo said, "I don't know myself. In town, I just heard it was a foreign film, so I went in. Afterwards, I told everyone the plot of the film and asked if they had ever seen a movie like it. No one said they'd ever seen it."

The Chief looked a little disappointed, "I would like to see this film."

One month later, one evening at dusk, Tharlo arrived at the County City carrying a pack. He walked straight into the hair salon.

The short-haired girl was giving a man a haircut. Tharlo sat on a stool to the side and looked at the short-haired girl in the mirror on the wall. The short-haired girl in the mirror laughed a bit but didn't greet Tharlo.

After the man had left, the short-haired girl looked at him from the mirror and said, "Your hair is dirty—it needs to be washed again."

Tharlo walked over and sat in the chair that the man had just been sitting in, then continued to look in the mirror at the short-haired girl.

Then the short-haired girl said, "What's wrong? Why is your face so white and pale?"

Tharlo placed the pack on a stand of hair-cutting tools and said, "This is 90,000 kuai."

The short-haired girl rested two hands on Tharlo's shoulders, looked at Tharlo's pale complexion in the mirror and said, "Relax, relax, just relax, and everything will be alright."

Tharlo did not speak. His complexion was still white and pale.

The short-haired girl said, "I'll wash your hair."

She applied shampoo on Tharlo's head and slowly kneaded it.

With the massaging, Tharlo relaxed. He slowly closed his eyes. His complexion recovered its normal appearance.

When Tharlo awoke, the short-haired girl was sitting beside him watching him.

The short-haired girl said, "You are too anxious! You fell asleep just now."

Tharlo glanced from side to side, his eyes looking as if he were in a dream.

The short-haired girls said, "I've already braided your braid."

Tharlo's expression was still as if in a dream or a daze.

The short-haired girl gave Tharlo a bottle of spring water and said, "Drink some water."

Tharlo opened the bottle and took several gulps.

Looking into Tharlo's eyes, the short-haired girl said, "Now you must do something for the two of us."

Tharlo looked into the short-haired girl's face and took another gulp of water.

The short-haired girl said, "Are you willing?"

Tharlo drank a large gulp which gurgled—*gugu*—as it rolled down his throat.

The short-haired girl said, "Your little braid is too noticeable. You have to cut it off."

Tharlo did not drink again. He looked at himself in the mirror.

The short-haired girl looked at Tharlo in the mirror and said, "Do you agree?"

Tharlo kept staring at his own face.

The short-haired girl said, "If you like long hair, I'll grow my hair long and comb it out into two long braids just for you to see alone."

Tharlo looked again and again at the face of the short-haired girl in the mirror.

The short-haired girl said, "Then I'll just cut it off and give you a shaved head. No one will recognize you."

Tharlo shut his eyes. The short-haired girl ran a few passes with the electric clippers and made Tharlo's head entirely clean-shaven. The little braid fell beside Tharlo's foot, still held by the red thread. Tharlo looked at it, bent down and picked up the little braid and put it into his pocket.

That night, the short-haired girl took Tharlo back to the same bar. Tharlo and the short-haired girl drank a lot of beer until they were as happy as could be. It was very late before they got to the place where the short-haired girl lived.

In the morning, when he woke up, Tharlo discovered the short-haired girl was gone, and, after he had searched everywhere, over and over, that the pack he'd brought with him was also gone.

Tharlo searched through the small County City for two days and two nights, but he did not find even a shadow of a trace of the short-haired girl.

Two days later, Tharlo went to the District Police Station. The Police Chief was talking to several officers about something.

Tharlo said, "Chief, I've come back."

The Chief looked at Tharlo's face for quite a while then suddenly said, "Hey, Little Braid, what happened to you? Where's your little braid?"

Tharlo said, "It's cut off."

The Chief said, "That's too bad."

Tharlo said, "Chief, now do you think I look like a bad person?"

The Chief said, "What do you mean?"

Tharlo said, "Aren't you able to see whether someone is a good person or a bad person with one glance?"

The Chief, laughing, said, "When you had your little braid you looked something like a bad person but now you don't look anything like a bad person. Instead you look just like a good person."

Tharlo said, "I'm afraid that if I were to die now it would be light as a feather."

The Chief, still laughing, said, "Aren't you just wanting to recite the sayings of Chairman Mao? I've already tested your memory. You don't need to recite it again."

Tharlo said, "It's too bad, too too bad, I cannot ever again be a good person like Zhang Side and die in serving the good of the people, someone whose death is as mighty as Mount Tai. I can die only like those bad people who die for Fascist traitors or die for those who exploit and oppress the people, whose death is lighter than a feather."

The Chief laughed and said, "Now that is a good application of the sayings of Chairman Mao."

Tharlo just said, "It's too bad, too too bad."

The Chief laughed and said to several officers who were working nearby, "*Ai*, can you believe this fellow can still recite many of the sayings of Chairman Mao?"

Several officers put down their work and looked at Tharlo with doubtful expressions, as if to say, "Him?"

The Chief said, "It looks like you'll have your eyes opened."

He turned again to Tharlo and said, "Recite 'To Serve the People' and let them expand their view of things."

Tharlo saw the expression of the officers. Without saying anything more he began to recite as if to himself,

"'Serve the People,' September 8, 1944. Mao Zedong.

"Our Communist Party and the Eighth Route and New Fourth Armies led by our Party are battalions of the revolution. These battalions of ours are wholly dedicated to the liberation of the people and work entirely in the people's interests. Comrade Zhang Side was in the ranks of these battalions. All men must die, but death can vary in its significance. The ancient Chinese writer Sima Qian said, 'Though death befalls all men alike, it may be weightier than Mount Tai or lighter than a feather.' To die for the people is weightier than Mount Tai but to work for the Fascists and die for the exploiters and oppressors is lighter than a feather. Comrade Zhang Side died for the people and his death is indeed weightier than Mount Tai...."

The officers all looked utterly stupefied as they watched Tharlo.

The Chief gestured with his hand for Tharlo to stop, then looked at the wide-eyed officers with their mouths dumbly open and said, "What's the matter—shocked? He can recite many of Chairman Mao's sayings."

The officers still stared dumbly at Tharlo.

The Chief said, "Alright, get back to work, we don't have all day."

Tharlo said, "Chief, I have become a bad person."

The Chief looked at Tharlo and said, "You don't become a bad person by getting your hair cut."

Then he said to one of the officers nearby, "Look in the recently finished identity cards, find his and give it to him."

The officer said, "What is his name?"

The Chief said, "Little Braid."

The officer said, "Huh?"

The Chief said, "*Hm*, no. That's his nickname."

He turned again to Tharlo and asked, "What was that real name of yours?"

Tharlo said, "Tharlo."

The Chief said, "Right, now I remember. It's Tharlo."

The officer looked in a file cabinet at the side of the room.

After a while the officer brought an identity card over and said, "Chief, is this it? It doesn't look much like him."

The Chief picked up the card and looked at it carefully. After studying it for some time he looked up at Tharlo and asked, "Will you not have a little braid anymore?"

Tharlo said, "No, I won't."

The Chief said, "Then you have to go back to the County City and get another picture taken. The way you look on the card is too different from the way you look now. When it's time, no one will be able to tell that the person on the card is the same person as you."

Tharlo wanted to say something more, but the Chief said, "Go right away, get it and bring it right back. We're very busy today."

MEN AND DOG

One winter evening, the west wind was blowing without pause, like a merciless flesh-eating demon, over the off-white grasslands. On this piece of the grasslands, three nomad households had planted their tents. Every year in winter, the three households, without any particular planning, and each on their own accord, inevitably came together at this one place.

That evening, however, something out of the ordinary happened in each of the three households. The head of the household to the east was a young man, and just today, he had happily welcomed his beloved bride from her distant home. A little after nightfall, he nervously extinguished the oil lamps and laid down with his bride in their bed of happiness.

In the household to the north, there were two, a mother and her daughter. The elderly mother was ill with a severe intestinal disease, suffering painfully. Since that morning, she had had a rising fever and had been on the verge of fainting a few times. Neighbors brought her medicine to quell her fever, and now they sat relaxed and at ease, talking with each other about this and that.

In the household to the south, there was a husband and a wife, who had been married for a little more than two years. Now, not only had nine months passed since she had conceived, but also ten more days. A few minutes after nightfall, an acute, unbearable pain came on, and she rolled back and forth again and again in her bed. If one looked at the shape and size of her body, it seemed like she would give birth that evening.

Translated from the Tibetan by Michael Monhart. Originally published in *Snow Flower (Gangs rgyan me tog)*, no. 2 (1997).

The west wind continued whistling painfully down from the western mountain ridges without obstruction. The three households' flocks of sheep were put in between their tents, while an ugly, dirty, nomad dog with a worn-out tail watched, standing guard over them.

Shortly after the arrival of midnight, not a single star was visible in the sky. Even the air, in all four directions, felt like it had completely stopped moving. Snowflakes began swirling along with a cold wind, falling from layers of clouds blowing to and fro. In a short time, the ground was completely white. The earth itself slipped peacefully into its own thoughts, as if mourning someone who had passed away.

The crying sound of a hungry wolf broke the calm of the evening, adding an air of utter terror that blew through the vacant world and made the hairs on people's bodies stand on end. Suddenly, the dog, his tail waving as if he had seen a stranger, raised his ears, rose up, and sped in the direction of the howling, hungry wolf—howling and barking now mixed together. Then, perhaps because it heard the barking of the dog, or perhaps for some other reason, the wolf stopped howling.

This made the dog anxious. Waving his short tail, he circled back around the flock of sheep, leaving countless paw prints in the snow. The nervous sheep bleated continuously. All of a sudden, hearing the cries of the wolf again, the dog stopped running and turned his ears towards a gap in the western mountains. The dog barked in that direction again and again, until he finally grew hoarse. It sounded like the wheezing of an old man suffering from tuberculosis. In the gap in the western mountain, all became silent and motionless as the cries of the hungry wolf gradually settled down. The dog relaxed, stretching his paws out before him and, panting, slowly began to recover. But all at once, the dog quickly got to its feet again and, after staring wide-eyed in each direction, ran with his tongue hanging out toward the tent to the east. Coming near the tent, the dog sat down on the ground, appeared to think for a moment, and then barked again and again, as if asking for something. At that moment though, the newly married husband and wife were caught up in a moment of pure bliss. It was impossible for them to sense at all what was happening outside. This went on for about an hour, and then the sound of the dog gradually became quieter. If one listened carefully, it sounded like a person sighing, and when that sound eventually ceased, all the surroundings also grew calm.

The darkness of the vast night obscured the mountains, valley, tents, and herds of sheep. The whole area appeared to be empty. However, in a little while, the cries of the hungry wolf shattered the overall tranquility of this emptiness again. At first, only one or two cries were heard, but they gradually grew more frequent. The dog, once again growing anxious, stood up and, listening to the cries of the hungry wolf, ran in the direction of the north tent. After arriving at the entrance, he stood before the tent, his tail shaking as before, barking and calling out. The old woman inside woke up. Moaning, she pulled both hands from under her sleeping blanket, while calling out her daughter's name. The daughter, also having awakened, now worried, was pacing back and forth near the old woman. Although she heard the barking, she did not have any time to pay attention to it, and only glancing at the door, let it be. The seconds passed one after the other, time moving along with the groans of the old woman. The barking of the dog gradually grew quieter. If one listened closely, it was just the same as someone lightly breathing. The cries of the hungry wolf ceased as well.

As before, the stars in the sky could not be seen. The snow continued to fall without pause. Once more, the ear-piercing cry of the hungry wolf was heard. Immediately, the dog raised his ears and with his tail shaking, circled anxiously around the flock of sheep and then quickly ran in the direction of the south tent. As soon as he got to the entrance of the tent, he stopped and, while barking and calling out, scratched the side of the tent with his paws. However, inside nothing could be heard but the relentless groans of intolerable pain and the sound of rushed footsteps. The dog howled and barked with all its might, but inside, the sounds of groaning and footsteps grew even more distinct. After a little time, the dog, as if tired, grew silent. Even if one listened attentively, nothing whatsoever could be heard.

Suddenly, the flock of sheep were swirling and milling about, filling the air with their bleating. The dog was barking amidst the rushing of the sheep. In the blink of an eye, the flock of sheep scattered, like shooting stars, in the four cardinal and four intermediate directions. The dog ran, sometimes cutting across the flock of sheep, sometimes circling them. In no time at all, he gathered the dispersed sheep together in one spot. His barking sounded far away until gradually nothing at all was heard. The cold, gusting wind had stopped and even the falling snow had ceased. Through the clouds, the moon showed a face of pity. The grasslands again grew tranquil. After a long time, the barking of the dog was heard again around the flock of sheep. However, it was not like before. If one listened closely, it sounded like the sad crying of an orphan abandoned in the snow.

It was past midnight. The youth woke pleasantly from the land of dreams. The old woman, as usual, gradually slipped into dreams, and nearby, the daughter was watching her with tired eyes. The pregnant woman now gave birth to a baby boy, and the tent filled with his cries. The father smiled with contentment and, gazing at his son's face, caressed him with his hand.

Once again, the endless barking of the dog reached everybody's ears. The constant barking made fearful doubts arise in their minds. They thought it was a bad omen of a coming drought. None of them, since the time they came to this world from their mothers' womb, had ever heard anything as frightening as the dog's dreadful cries. A fierce hatred arose in them. They felt angry with the dog, with its hairy, ugly shape. No one wanted to continue to listen to such terrifying barking. And so, each of them, having taken up a hard, thick piece of wood, emerged from their doors and drew near the dog. Under the cold light of the moon, they stood on either side of the dog, staring at each other with cold eyes, not uttering a word. Under the cold light of the moon, they saw each other holding a piece of wood in their hands. As soon as he heard the footsteps of the people, the dog stopped barking. The four cardinal and four intermediate directions grew as quiet as a cemetery. Yet, the dog's barking began again, immediately shattering the quiet. They all focused now on the dog, lying on the snow. First, the man who had become a father angrily raised his arms up and powerfully struck the dog's back. After letting out a cry of unbearable pain, the dog became silent. Following right after, the daughter of the old woman forcefully hit the dog's neck. The dog slowly raised its head and, with unbelieving eyes, stared at its masters for a moment, a single tear falling to the ground. Finally, the young man, who had just been married that day, raised his well-muscled arms high and, with all his power, violently struck the center of the dog's brain. The dog, its head slumped to the ground, remained motionless. They stood there, not looking at each other. The young man kicked the top of the motionless dog. Then the daughter of the old woman and the father of the boy followed suit. After that, all returned to their own tents.

In the chill of the next morning, a red sun slowly rose above the border between the earth and sky, and in the snow all was clear and vivid. When the sun had risen a bit above the horizon, they went out: first was the young man who had just got married, rubbing his eyes; after that, the daughter of the old woman, moving sluggishly; finally, the father of the boy, an unrestrainable smile on his tired face. After greeting each other, they slowly went in the direction of the flock of sheep. When they had gone about five or six steps, they noticed a large number of marks of the dog's paw prints in the snow. After that, they saw fallen sheep everywhere and all around them blood. Dumbfounded, they ran up and down in the snow. Finally, their eyes focused together on the collapsed body of the dog in the snow. With heavy footsteps they moved slowly in his direction. After they had drawn near, all were taken back by the scene in front of their eyes. One of the dog's legs had completely vanished and the wound was covered in blood. Along with that, clearly arranged on the neck and spine, were the sharp teeth marks of a wolf. His short, worn-out tail was almost completely bitten off, attached by only a shred of skin. They could not keep looking at the crushed, bloody corpse of the dog. Recalling last night's pitiful barking, little by little they began to understand what had happened.

Drops of blood in the snow stretched out before them, looking like the little hearts of children. They slowly bent down and each picked up, in their hands, a single drop of blood on the snow that looked like a child's heart. They stared at the drops, reflecting, not moving at all. One cannot say whether the expressions on their faces were of satisfaction or sorrow.

AFTERNOON

Young Wangbum woke up, opened the window and, looking outside, said, "The moon light is truly beautiful this evening!"

He remembered he had a date with Dolma that night, so he got up quickly. He expected that Dolma would be waiting for him at that very moment, waiting to tell him some good news.

When he was outside and about to lock his door, he suddenly remembered something and reentered the house again. He went to get his long ladder.

This was from experience. Sometimes when he had gone to see Dolma at midnight, he had found her deeply asleep and had to wait all night in vain. The way they usually dated was that he would go to the back of her house in the middle of the night and throw some pebbles at her window. Upon hearing this, she would come down and open the door quietly. But this way of seeing each other had its moments of risk too. Sometimes, Dolma would fall into a deep sleep, and he would throw pebbles all night to no avail. Other times, he would attract the attention of her family's big, black dog, who would continually bark at him. As a result, Dolma's father would wake up and, thinking that a thief had entered the house, point here and there with his flashlight, frightening Young Wangbum nearly to death. That is why, later on, Young Wangbum decided to take his own ladder, so that it did not matter how deeply asleep Dolma was, he could always get to her room through the wall of the courtyard behind the house.

Translated from the Chinese by Patricia Schiaffini-Vedani. Originally published in *Fragrant Grass (Fang cao)*, no. 2 (2009).

As Young Wangbum walked along a small pathway by the farm fields, he looked up and thought, "The moon tonight is truly bright, so bright I cannot even open my eyes to look at it." A cool and refreshing breeze blew in his face and made him feel very comfortable, so he finished his thought, "But tonight's breeze is so nice!"

From the narrow pathway in the fields, Young Wangbum took a wide dirt road. On it he saw a snake pushing its way through, flicking its tongue and making hissing noises. He came to a sudden halt because he was afraid of snakes—just looking at it terrified him. The snake also stopped to look at him, but left after a short while. He looked at the place where the snake had disappeared, fearing it might return suddenly, but it did not.

Carrying the ladder on his shoulder, Young Wangbum dashed along the road, making clouds of dust. His footsteps were light, as if he were not carrying anything on his shoulder. He slowed down when he saw Kyaba, from the neighboring village, approaching from the other side of the road. Kyaba also had a girlfriend in this village, and sometimes they would bump into each other in the fields at midnight. Once he even lent the ladder to Kyaba. For this reason they got along well. There was a period of time when Young Wangbum was a bit depressed because some of the boys in that village, furious that he was going out with Dolma, were always looking for excuses to fight with him. At that time, Kyaba had advised him not to take it to heart. Kyaba had said to him, "Dolma, such a beautiful girl, is in love with you, what is the point of being sad? If I were you, I would be thrilled." Young Wangbum thought that Kyaba was right. Those boys acted like that only because they were jealous.

When Kyaba stood in front of Young Wangbum, he greeted him and asked where Young Wangbum was going. But Young Wangbum gave an answer to a different topic, "Just now there was a snake crossing the dirt road under the moonlight."

Kyaba looked at the sky and then said, "I am asking you where you are going."

Young Wangbum thought a bit and said, "That snake even stopped to look at me. I started running when it left. I am afraid of snakes." Kyaba looked behind Young Wangbum. Young Wangbum calmly said, "The snake is gone already."

Kyaba looked him in the eye and asked, "I meant, where are you going at this time of the day?"

Young Wangbum thought the question was a bit strange. Usually, when he met Kyaba at this time of day, Kyaba would always have an enigmatic look in his face, but tonight Kyaba looked at him like any other person saying hello. Although he thought it was a bit odd, he replied, "Of course I am going to meet Dolma."

Kyaba looked at him in awe, "What? What did you just say?"

Thinking Kyaba had not heard him well, he repeated, "Well, I am going to see my Dolma, of course."

This time Kyaba seemed to understand what he said and laughed. Then, looking at the ladder on Young Wangbum's shoulder, asked, "So, what is the ladder for?"

Young Wangbum first looked around and then talked to him in a secretive voice, "It is with this ladder that I can climb up to Dolma's room. Don't you remember, you also used it to meet your girlfriend?" Kyaba laughed again. Young Wangbum thought it was a strange laugh so he asked, "What are you laughing at?" But Kyaba continued laughing without answering. Also smiling, Young Wangbum said, "If you want to borrow it now, I can go there a bit later."

Young Wangbum's tone still sounded secretive, so Kyaba laughed even more and all of a sudden said, "You idiot!"

Hearing this made Young Wangbum unhappy. He put down the ladder and said, "I kindly offer my ladder to you and, to my surprise, you call me an idiot!"

Kyaba, with a straight face, said, "You *are* an idiot."

Young Wangbum, very upset now, pushed Kyaba and said, "I dare you to say it again!"

Kyaba, looking pretty mad too, shouted, "You are an idiot, a big idiot!"

Young Wangbum landed a heavy blow to Kyaba's head, who fell into a water ditch. "Say it again if you dare," said Young Wangbum. Kyaba, lying on the ditch, did not budge, but did not repeat the insult either. Young Wangbum picked up his ladder from the ground and said, "Had you not called me an idiot, I would have gladly lent you the ladder." Upon saying this, he walked away carrying his ladder, but after walking fifteen or twenty steps, he heard a noise coming from behind. Kyaba was standing up in the gutter with some difficulty. Looking at Kyaba, Young Wangbum could not help but smile. Then he heard Kyaba's voice saying, "You are an idiot!" Young Wangbum's smile disappeared and he was about to go back to give Kyaba another blow but, thinking it over again, decided not to, as Dolma would surely be waiting for him now. He smiled again and said, "Dolma is waiting for me now. Tomorrow in the light of the day, I will look for you to settle this score." This said, he put his ladder on his shoulder and left. Behind him, he could hear the echoes of Kyaba's curse words.

When he passed by the wheat field of Widow Droltso, he saw her carrying her child on her back. She was behind two donkeys pulling a stone roller over the highland barley. Young Wangbum thought, "Such a hardworking widow. She continues to work at night, under such a big moon, to finish the day's work." At this time, her baby began to cry.

Seeing Young Wangbum outside the field, the widow said, "My baby needs to nurse. Come over and let's have a cup of tea."

Young Wangbum did not have time to drink before leaving his house, and since he felt a bit thirsty, he left the ladder beside the wheat field and walked to her house. At this time, Young Wangbum saw the widow's black cat carrying a fat black rat in his mouth. He had snatched it out of the watering hole at the foot of the wall. The cat arched half of his body and yowled in fear, as if somebody would take away his black rat. That rat, still alive, was struggling with all its might inside the black cat's mouth. Blinking its little eyes, the rat was making squeaking noises as if asking Young Wangbum to save its life. He did not feel any empathy for the rat though. One rat at his house had bitten to pieces a Buddhist *thangka* painting that had belonged to his family for generations and a volume of scriptures his father had used to teach him when he was a child. For this reason, he bought poison and even got a cat, but nothing was good enough to deal with that crazy rat.

The black rat inside the mouth of the black cat, trapped, continued looking at Young Wangbum, as if guessing what he would do next. Young Wangbum praised the cat out loud, "You are the best of cats! In a black night, a black cat catches such a fat black rat. You certainly have an extraordinary ability!" Even before Young Wangbum was done saying this, the black cat, still holding the fat rat in his mouth, moved backwards from the watering hole and ran away. Young Wangbum—his mouth opened in disappointment—stopped singing the cat's praises and went to the widow's place.

Widow Droltso, breastfeeding her baby, poured a cup of tea for Young Wangbum. Although Droltso was a widow, she was still very young. She had married at seventeen, become a widow at eighteen, and given birth to this child at nineteen. She was very beautiful, and many boys from the village liked her. Widow Droltso, however, only had eyes for Young Wangbum. She was feeding the baby while watching Young Wangbum drinking his tea. Seeing that he had already finished with his bowl of tea, she poured him another bowl and said, "White Dolma is truly a fortunate girl!"

White Dolma was Dolma's nickname. Her skin was very white, so the boys and girls in the village called her White Dolma. Young Wangbum began to say, "You are very fortunate too," but then he realized that did not seem quite right, so he just looked at her in silence.

Widow Droltso looked at him with deep feeling, saying, "Would you be my husband?" She had told Young Wangbum such things before, and he had always pretended not to hear. She continued, "As long as you agree to be my husband, you do not need to lift a finger around the house. I will cook for you whatever you want to eat. If you want to eat meat you can eat those few sheep of mine. All I want is for you to be with me every day." Upon hearing this, a smile appeared on Young Wangbum's face. Seeing him smiling, she continued, "This child will be yours, a child that is not lame or blind ... what can be better under the Heavens? I'll make you the happiest man in the village."

Young Wangbum replied, "I don't deserve all these promises of yours, my fate is not that good. But I do have a favor to ask from you, although I am not sure if it is possible."

Looking at him passionately, she answered, "Everything I have is yours. If you want, I can give myself to you right now."

Young Wangbum, a bit anxious, replied clumsily, "Can you lend me that black cat of yours for a few days?"

Widow Droltso suddenly put the baby down and threw herself at him saying, "I lend myself to you for a whole life!"

At that moment the baby began to cry, and Young Wangbum pushed Widow Droltso away, nervously saying, "Quickly, the baby is crying, why don't you feed him?" Taking advantage of Widow Droltso feeding the baby, Young Wangbum stood up, took his ladder, and left in a hurry.

He heard her shouting in the back, "I give you the cat. He's always chasing rats. It's disgusting."

In order to get to Dolma's house it was necessary to pass by Uncle Tonpa's home. Just as he was about to reach Uncle Tonpa's house, a shaky tractor passed by him almost knocking his ladder off. He quickly moved aside, giving way for the tractor. The clunky sounds that thing made annoyed him. The tractor was carrying some boys and girls who waved at him. Fearing they would guess he was going to meet Dolma, he quickly looked down, pretending not to see them.

The sound of the tractor was disappearing when he finally got to Uncle Tonpa's home. Uncle Tonpa was sitting on an old rug next to an outside wall of his home, reciting the Om mantra while moving his prayer beads. Seeing Young Wangbum passing by, Uncle Tonpa said, "You truly will make a good son-in-law! At this time of the day you are still going to help others."

Young Wangbum thought it was strange to see the old man out alone this late at night. But then he understood. He thought that today must be a special day—that was surely the reason why Dolma chose tonight to give him the good news. "Grandpa, you are praying, huh?" he said smiling.

Uncle Tonpa answered, "We old people have to store up some provisions for the next life, otherwise how are we going to be able to get on the road when Death arrives? Every bit we can pray now counts."

Young Wangbum thought this old man really knew how to pick his praying time. Praying under such an enchanting moon would help him accumulate much more merit than his usual prayers.

Seeing that Young Wangbum was still carrying the ladder on his shoulder, Uncle Tonpa asked him, "Why don't you put down the ladder and sit down and talk to me for a while?" The boy did so and sat beside the old man. "What a great thing if, in the future, I could have a good son-in-law like you," Uncle Tonpa said. Young Wangbum remained silent, so the old man went on, saying, "What's wrong with being my son-in-law? I only have a daughter, and soon I will be joining the dead. You could be the owner of this house. Do as you please, say what you please, without paying attention to others. Isn't this a good life for a man?" These words made Young Wangbum feel out of breath. Uncle Tonpa had said such things to him many times before. The old man's daughter was also named Dolma, like the other Dolma in Young Wangbum's heart, but her skin was darker, so the boys and girls from the village had given her the nickname of Black Dolma—exactly the opposite of his girlfriend, White Dolma. Black Dolma was twenty-five years old. Uncle Tonpa did not want to marry her out, and none of the village boys wanted to come to live at his house as his son-in-law, so she was still waiting alone at home.

Young Wangbum continued to remain silent, so the old man went on, "What is so special about being with White Dolma? She has an elder brother and a younger brother, so surely there is nothing you can fish out from that family. On top of it, you are always helping them do so many things, this way aren't you working for somebody else's family? You are a carefree orphan, why should you bother? If you come to my house, I will give you all of my family's rights."

Young Wangbum finally said, "I will not become her parents' son-in-law. I will marry her into my family."

Uncle Tonpa laughed coldly, "*Ha!* Do you think they will give you White Dolma? And what will you marry her with, since you have no money?"

Young Wangbum smiled and replied, "Her elder brother has just come back from town to discuss the issue of our marriage. She said that today, by this time of the day, they will have come to a decision. That is why I am heading there now. As long as they agree to our marriage, I have the means to marry her with dignity."

At that moment, Uncle Tonpa's big yellow dog approached slowly. Usually, when Young Wangbum was on his way to see Dolma and carrying his ladder, the dog would hide around Uncle Tonpa's house, waiting to attack him; so he feared and hated this old yellow dog. As the dog was approaching, Young Wangbum was ready to stand up and run, but the old man, smiling, reassured him, "He will not bite you. He already sees you as a family member." The dog did not look as vicious as usual, so Young Wangbum stayed seated. The old yellow dog earnestly licked Young Wangbum's leather shoes. "I talked to him about you yesterday," said Uncle Tonpa, smiling strangely. Young Wangbum took a glance at the dog, got his ladder and left. Uncle Tonpa, still laughing, shouted behind him, "Truly an ideal son-in-law!"

He was almost at Dolma's home when he saw in the distance her family's big black dog running in his direction. He used to hate this big black dog too, because every time he visited Dolma at night, the dog would follow him, barking non-stop. Once its barking even alerted Dolma's father, who came out with two big stones in his hands looking in the direction of the dog's barking. Young Wangbum had to flee and did not manage to see Dolma. Later, the dog finally became his friend because Young Wangbum decided to feed him some tasty treats during the day.

The dog approached him wagging its tail. Young Wangbum emptied his pockets looking for something to feed the dog, but he did not find anything. Although the dog looked a bit disappointed, it nonetheless walked ahead of Young Wangbum as if showing him the way. From a distance he saw that the door to Dolma's house was wide open, and he thought this was a bit strange. In front of the door there were chickens, pigs, sheep, and the like, all roaming freely. Usually at this time the door was closed shut. He was not sure why this was not the case tonight.

The dog entered the courtyard. Young Wangbum, carrying his ladder, hesitated for a moment but decided to enter as well. When he crossed to the second courtyard door, he heard a lot of voices, so he raised his head to look. From the kitchen window he saw Dolma's parents, her younger brother, and her elder brother, who had arrived from the city, discussing something. He blushed in embarrassment. Being seen by your girlfriend's family when you were trying to have a date with her was the most awkward of situations, especially today when the whole family was there. He wanted to sneak out before they had noticed his presence, but at that moment, the dog barked toward the window. Dolma's father, seeing Young Wangbum there, stood up and said, "You came to help even at this time. We are truly grateful." Young Wangbum had no choice but to stand there embarrassed. Noticing he was carrying a ladder, Dolma's father asked, "Why are you carrying a ladder? We have ladders here too."

"I thought it could be useful, being fall harvest and all," uttered Young Wangbum after a brief silence.

"Oh, that is so thoughtful of you! You are a good boy. It looks like our Dolma has a good eye."

Dolma's elder brother came out of the kitchen, took a pack of Red Pagoda Mountain cigarettes out from his jacket's pocket and offered the pack to Young Wangbum, saying, "Take it, smoke these. I brought them from the city. The best tobacco in town." Young Wangbum refused, but after a moment he took it. "I've heard you help our family a lot. Many thanks," the elder brother said, lighting a cigarette. Young Wangbum acted as if he did not know what to do or say.

Looking at his appearance, Dolma's face turned red, and she quickly came out. Seeing her approach, her elder brother decided to enter the house again. Flushed, she got in front of Young Wangbum and said, "Why do you come at this hour? And carrying your ladder!"

Feeling a bit wronged, he replied, "Didn't we agree to see each other at this time?"

Impatient and angry, the girl stared at him, "You fool! It is just the afternoon. The sun is still above our heads, and my family is just now discussing our relationship."

Young Wangbum, a bit confused, and seeing Dolma's flushed face, did not know what to do. After a while he said, "In that case, I will go back and sleep a bit more."

EIGHT SHEEP

Gyalo brought his sheep there to graze pretty much every day. He was a cute boy of twelve or thirteen years of age, with matted hair and silly looks. He always wore a short leather jacket. The leather jacket had been made by his mother the previous year, so it was a bit small and old now, but he still liked to wear it. He even wore it long into the summer when it was very hot. Other young shepherds asked him if he did not have summer clothes, but he did not answer. That was not it. He did have several nice summer garments that he liked to wear. But this leather jacket was made by Mother's beloved hands, especially for him. Mother had died unexpectedly in the spring, so it was very hard for him to take off his leather jacket—wearing it, he felt like Mother was beside him. Later on, he finally had to change into his summer clothes. He chose his favorite denim outfit. He hid his leather jacket carefully in a trunk. He knew nobody would make a new jacket for him for this year's New Year's celebration. Now that the weather was getting colder again, he started wearing his leather jacket once more. He was sure he could wear it for several more years.

The sheep grazed lazily on the grass, bathed by the warm golden rays of the midday sun. Every day at this time, Gyalo chewed yak jerky. When his mother was alive, she always put some in his bag, so he could snack on it at any time. He kept the habit of bringing it with him, but he liked to eat it only on schedule. He would take out the yak jerky to eat

Translated from the Chinese by Patricia Schiaffini-Vedani. Originally published in *Fragrant Grass (Fang cao)*, no. 2 (2009).

when the noon sun was right on top of his head, his body casting only a tiny shadow on the ground.

When he was done eating, it was his habit to take a drink of water from his canteen and lay down on his back for a while. Sometimes he would stare directly at the sun, even though his eyes would hurt badly. After lunch, a spell of drowsiness would assault him, and occasionally he would take a nap, although Mother had repeatedly exhorted him not to sleep on the grass. She had tried to frighten him, saying that bugs could crawl into his ears and eat his brain. She even told him a story:

"Once upon a time, there was this poor little shepherd who would take his dog with him to the mountains to let his sheep out to pasture. He liked to sleep while tending to his sheep. One day, when he returned home, he felt an excruciating pain in his ear. Nothing he did could alleviate it. In the middle of the night, he heard voices, so he opened his eyes. He saw his shepherd dog talking to the cat. The cat said, 'I feel terrible seeing our master in such pain.' 'I am sad too, the master is so nice to us,' the dog answered. The cat asked, 'Isn't there any way to treat this illness?' 'What the master has is not a disease. Some bugs entered his ear when he was sleeping on the mountain. It hurts so much because they are now eating his brain,' the dog said. 'Is there no way to make it better then?' the cat asked. The dog replied, 'The way to get rid of them is quite simple. You splash water on the ground inside the house, make a fire, and hit a drum close to his ears. Those bugs will think they are hearing the thunders of spring, and they will come out. Then you just need to smash them one by one and it is solved. It is just too bad we are animals, and we cannot tell these things to the master.' The cat said, 'Yes, it is too bad. I hope the master recovers soon.' The young shepherd quickly did what the dog said and cured himself."

Thinking about this story made Gyalo very happy because Mother had told it to him. He was not sure whether to believe it or not, but he was still a bit scared, so he would only take a nap when he was unbearably sleepy, and after stuffing his ears tightly with wool.

After his sleepiness passed, he looked far away, captivated. Although the scenery in front of him was always the same, he still loved to gaze at the distance, as if the view could change every day.

The boy could hear the bleats of about a dozen sheep grazing in the distance. He looked far away, and his expression turned sad, in a way that was hard to describe. As the fall winds blew their desolation around, the grass nearby had already turned brown. From time to time, a few young lambs circled around the herd or ambled through the grass. Gyalo moved his body a little bit, and his expression changed. A trembling baby lamb, who was wandering in the meadow, looked at the boy several times and then ran back to the flock. An ewe, probably his mother, approached the baby and smelled his tail, but when he got under her belly to suck milk, she kicked him away and left. Staring at them, the boy's expression changed again. The baby bleated several times and the ewe came back. Smelling his head, she finally allowed him to suck milk. Gyalo smiled.

A rustling noise came from Gyalo's left side. This alarmed several sheep in the underbrush, and they hurriedly retreated. The boy followed the noise with his gaze. A rabbit came out of the weeds and disappeared in a flash. Shaking in fear, the sheep looked at the moving grass in the spot from where the rabbit had come. Looking at them, the boy took out a piece of yak jerky, put it in his mouth, and began to chew on it. He looked across the meadow. There, several sheep were lying down; some were standing. They looked as if they had eaten their fill. A small one slowly approached to smell the jerky in his hand, showing interest in trying a bit. Patting his mouth he said, "You cannot eat this. It is not tasty." The little lamb seemed to understand and placidly left. Gyalo put the rest of the meat in his mouth and chewed on it.

The sounds of steps came to him from the grass behind the wire fence. Without much interest, the boy turned his head to look. That piece of land did not belong to him. He could only tend his flock on his own land. Ever since the land had been divided and assigned to each family, the vast grasslands had been cut in disarray. Every family had installed an iron-wire fence to block the entrance of others' animals into their property.

Although the sounds of the steps came closer and closer, Gyalo could not see anything. He stood up to watch, and this time he saw someone coming down from the top of the slope. The man approaching wore a wide-brimmed hat that covered his face. The boy could not see him clearly, but he saw that the man was carrying a big bag on his back. The man piqued Gyalo's curiosity, so he stopped chewing on his jerky to look more carefully. By the way he walked, the man looked a bit tired, but he still had a strong figure. He continued walking without lifting his head, which intrigued Gyalo. He tried to recall if he knew somebody with a similar physique, but he could not think of anybody who looked like that. He gazed at him with even more interest.

The man finally arrived at the wire fence, took off his hat, and lifted his head. To Gyalo's surprise, he was a blond, blue-eyed foreigner. Gyalo had seen foreigners only on television, never in person, so he felt a bit anxious. Even the baby lamb sucking milk stopped to look with novelty at the newcomer.

Unconsciously, the boy opened his mouth wide, unable to utter a word. The foreigner said something in English and gave a friendly smile. Gyalo, his mouth still open, just stared at the man.

The foreigner jumped over the fence and walked toward Gyalo, saying hello in poor Tibetan. The boy, even more surprised, kept silent. The foreigner repeated his heavily accented "hello." After a little while, Gyalo spat the yak jerky from his mouth and also said, "Hello." The foreigner produced an amiable smile.

The noon sunshine falling straight down on them was unpleasant to the eyes. As if the boy had suddenly thought of something, he looked down to see the shadow of the foreigner. The man's shadow was almost identical to his, so Gyalo relaxed a little and smiled. Seeing this, the foreigner smiled back at him. His smile was different from all the other smiles Gyalo had seen.

"Where are you from?" asked the boy curiously.

The foreigner shrugged his shoulders and replied in English, "My apologies but I only know that one word in Tibetan."

Seeing no reaction in Gyalo's face, he said the same sentence in not very proficient Mandarin. The boy's expression was still clueless.

The foreigner added in Mandarin, "Don't you speak Mandarin?" Still, that blank look from Gyalo.

"I guess not," said the foreigner, shrugging his shoulders again. He put down his big backpack and sat beside the boy. Gyalo was on guard to see what the foreigner would do next, but the man just sat there, sometimes looking at Gyalo and sometimes looking at the grasslands where the sheep grazed.

Being so close to the Westerner made Gyalo even more curious about him. Staring at him carefully for a while, Gyalo asked again, "Where are you from?"

The foreigner made a helpless gesture and, looking across to the sheep, said, "You have so many of them!"

The baby lamb who was sucking milk came over, apparently already full. The ewe came too and, after sniffing around, returned to grazing on the grass. With a tender gaze, the boy held the baby in his arms.

Caressing the baby lamb's head gently, the foreigner said, "It is truly great to see somebody else in the grasslands!"

Gyalo thought he was talking about his sheep, and he nodded.

The foreigner got excited and said, "Did you understand what I just said?"

A bit suspicious, the boy shook his head. Disappointed, the foreigner shook his head as well.

The boy began teasing the baby lamb, but after playing for a while, the lamb got restless and left.

Looking at the baby lamb as it left, the foreigner said, in a mix of English and Mandarin, "I've been here for almost a year now. I came to study Chinese at a university. I can already read and speak a little. I am very interested in Tibetan culture."

Gyalo was not sure what to do after the foreigner had said so much, so he just took a piece of yak jerky out and began to chew on it.

"It is so nice to be able to talk to somebody!" said the foreigner, looking at the boy.

Gyalo looked at the cracked lips of the foreigner. "Eat," he said, offering the man some jerky.

The man immediately understood what the boy meant. With a grateful look in his eyes, he took a piece of jerky and put it in his mouth. After chewing on it for a while, he gave a thumb's up and said, "Very good!"

A smile appeared on Gyalo's face when he saw the thumb's up, as he understood that the foreigner was pleased.

After he had finished eating, the foreigner showed the boy his digital watch. "Have you seen one of these?" he asked.

Gyalo nodded, as if he had understood the question.

Excited, the foreigner pointed to his watch and continued saying in English, "Look, today is the twenty-eighth. I have been in the grasslands for more than twenty days."

Gyalo nodded again.

The foreigner was even more excited. "It is so nice to be able to talk to somebody!" he repeated.

After a pause, in a serious tone, he explained, "I wanted to understand Tibetan culture, so I came alone to the Tibetan areas to experience it on-site first and then engage in deeper research."

After saying this, he looked at Gyalo. The boy looked back with a vacant expression on his face, then began chewing again.

The foreigner felt helpless. He thought for a moment and then took a book from his bag. He showed the boy the image of the Statue of Liberty and said, "I am an American. This is the famous Statue of Liberty." He looked at Gyalo again. The boy was looking at the statue. For a moment, it looked as if Gyalo was thinking about something, but then he regained his blank expression and continued chewing on his meat.

Turning the page, the foreigner pointed to a picture of New York's many skyscrapers and continued saying in English, "This is my hometown, New York. Other people think this is Heaven on Earth, but I do not like it there. I cannot stand life there. I love it here: the vast grasslands, the pure sky. I always think life is elsewhere."

He looked at the boy again. Gyalo was looking at the picture of New York with the same vacant look.

With a tone of sadness in his voice, the foreigner continued, "I know you do not understand what I am saying. It does not matter. I guess I am saying all these things to myself."

Still chewing, it seemed Gyalo was not paying attention to what the foreigner was saying.

Suddenly realizing something, the foreigner pointed to a pin on his shirt and said, "Do you know this?"

Gyalo looked at his chest and saw a souvenir badge of the Potala Palace.

"The Potala. You know it?" the foreigner asked again.

The boy swallowed the yak jerky and said happily, "That is the Potala."

"This time you understood what I said!" The foreigner got excited.

The boy seemed to like the badge very much and examined it carefully. At home he had a big painting of the Potala Palace. Mother used to say that was the place she wanted to visit the most. She said she would surely go to the Potala on a pilgrimage in her lifetime. But she died before being able to make it there. Gyalo felt very sorry about this. The boy wanted to say these things to the foreigner, but then thought there was no point in saying all that. The foreigner would probably not understand it anyway.

The sound of a lamb interrupted Gyalo's thoughts. He looked in the direction of the noise and saw a ewe giving birth on the grass, so he went to her. The ewe was lying on her side on the grass. The baby's head was already out of her body. Gyalo's experienced hands helped her give birth. The Westerner also came over to watch. Sorry to see how much the ewe was struggling to give birth, he seemed eager to give Gyalo a hand, yet he did not know what to do.

When the baby finally came out, the amniotic fluid spilled all over the grass. Its body was covered with a sticky layer. The ewe stood up, shaking, and lovingly cleaned the little lamb with her tongue.

The baby, still on the ground, struggled in vain to stand up. Gyalo told the Westerner happily, "In a little while, he will be able to stand on his own!" The Westerner smiled, even though he did not understand what Gyalo had said.

Gyalo cleaned his hands with dry grass and returned to the place where he was sitting before. A black-headed baby lamb came over to Gyalo, who held him in his arms.

After looking at the newborn for a while, the Westerner came over to sit down by Gyalo again. Gyalo took another piece of jerky and offered it to him. The Westerner took it, nodded thankfully, and began chewing on it. He realized that Gyalo's expression had changed—he now looked very sad.

After a little while, the Westerner extended his thumb and said happily, "Very good jerky. You are very good too." Gyalo's tears rolled down his face. The Westerner quickly asked in Chinese, "What's the matter?"

Gyalo said in Tibetan, "I was about to have a hundred lambs in my herd, but last night some wolves broke through the metal fence and attacked my flock, killing eight of my lambs."

The Westerner, in awe, looked at Gyalo crying. Gyalo went on saying, "My mother and I really wanted our herd to reach a hundred lambs this year. But last night those merciless wolves ate eight of them."

As if he had suddenly understood something, the Westerner said in English, "I see, something very sad must have happened to you. Is that so?"

Gyalo went on crying and speaking, without paying attention to what he said. "The mother of this black-headed lamb I am holding was among those killed last night. He looks so sad."

Trying to comfort Gyalo, the Westerner jokingly said, "Are you in love with a girl who does not return your feelings?"

Seeing the Westerner's lively expression, Gyalo smiled too, "Maybe I should not worry. Didn't we just see a baby lamb being born? My flock will get to a hundred lambs next year."

The Westerner thought that his words had played a role in cheering Gyalo up, "Wasn't I right? Maybe you did not tell her enough pleasantries. You have to say nice things to make her happy."

The sound of a motorcycle came from a distance. Gyalo and the Westerner looked in that direction. Even some lambs stopped grazing to listen to the noise. They could not see the road but they could see the cloud of dust. Its roar could be heard coming closer and closer. After a little while, the motorcycle left the main road and approached them, still leaving behind a lot of dust. Gyalo, the Westerner, and a group of lambs continued observing the scene until the motorcycle arrived and stopped on the side of the road by the metal-wire fence. The driver was a middle-aged man wearing a sheepskin robe.

After securing the motorcycle, he asked Gyalo, "Who is that person by your side?"

"I am not sure," Gyalo said. "A blond foreigner. I had only seen them on TV before and now one is sitting right here. It is very strange."

"You should be vigilant," the man replied. "I am not sure why, but in recent years there have been more and more of these foreigners around the grasslands."

Considering what he had just heard, he nodded and looked at the foreigner. The foreigner gave a friendly smile and said hello in Tibetan to the newcomer. The man looked at him in awe and said, "This guy even knows how to speak Tibetan."

"I think he only knows how to say that word," answered Gyalo, looking again at the foreigner. Exchanging his surprised look for a smile, the man said, "Oh, that's better! I was worried he had understood what we were just saying."

"He does not understand," replied Gyalo.

The man took from the motorcycle bag a bundle of newspapers tied with a string. He asked Gyalo, "Is the Village Head at home?"

The boy stood up, approached the man and replied, "He is home. I saw him early this morning when I went to report last night's wolf attack on my flock."

"Oh, there have been several attacks by wolves recently. We should watch out. How many lambs did you lose?" asked the man.

Gyalo's voice turned sad. "Eight," he said.

"Eight is not that much," said the man without giving it too much thought. Then he added, "A friend of mine lost more than thirty last year. Those wolves were vicious. They killed them all and left without eating a bite."

A smile appeared in Gyalo's face. "From now on I will follow my herd, that way nothing bad will happen to them," he said. He turned and, pointing to the new baby lamb, added, "That one was just born."

The man looked in the direction Gyalo was pointing. The baby lamb was struggling to stand up. He smiled and said, "When it grows up it will surely be a wonderful lamb!" This made Gyalo very happy.

The man threw the newspaper in Gyalo's direction and said, "This newspaper is only distributed every two weeks. Make sure you give this to the Village Head. It has a lot of news."

"Don't worry. I'll give it to him," replied the boy.

The foreigner had been observing them the whole time. Seeing that the man was ready to leave, he approached them as if he had suddenly thought of something to say. "Do you speak Chinese?" he asked the man.

The man stared blankly for a while and finally replied in poor Mandarin, "I don't speak Chinese."

"But you just spoke in Chinese!" said the Westerner in astonishment.

The man paused for a while and added, "I just know that sentence."

The foreigner did not say anything else.

The man said bye to Gyalo in Tibetan, turned on his motorcycle, and left, following the road and leaving a layer of dust behind him.

The newspaper bundle was on the grass between Gyalo and the Westerner. Both of them followed the man on the motorcycle with their eyes.

When the sight and the roar of the bike finally disappeared, they heard a bleating. They turned and saw that the baby lamb was finally able to stand up, although he did not look very stable. He swayed back and forth and fell down again.

Gyalo heard a noise and looked to the foreigner, who was staring at something in the newspaper. Gyalo looked at the newspaper too. There was a black and white image that attracted his attention. In the image, a plane was crashing into a skyscraper, thick smoke surrounding the building. Below the picture there were lots of Chinese characters. Gyalo could not understand what was written there, so he lifted his head only to see the foreigner still looking at the picture, his eyes full of tears. Still crying and unable to utter a single word, he lifted his eyes from the newspaper and fixed them on Gyalo's face.

The boy was not sure what was wrong. After looking at the foreigner for a while he tried to comfort him, "Something very bad must have happened to you. Don't cry."

The foreigner said in English, "Something terrible happened in my hometown the eleventh day of this month. So many of my loved ones live there, and I did not know a thing." His tears fell again. Gyalo did not know what to say. The foreigner hugged the boy and cried loudly, without feeling shame. At first, Gyalo felt uncomfortable, but he slowly relaxed and let the foreigner cry loudly on his shoulder.

From behind them, the boy heard the bleats of the baby lamb. He turned his head and saw the baby standing well, wagging his tale and looking for his mother's udder.

Gyalo pushed the foreigner a couple of times. The foreigner was still crying. Gyalo pushed him a bit harder, and this time the foreigner looked at him. Gyalo pointed so that the foreigner could see the little lamb. The lamb was kneeling down on the grass drinking milk from his mother.

The foreigner stopped crying and looked at the baby lamb in a daze. After a while, he picked up his backpack and said to Gyalo in English, "I have to leave immediately. I have to go back home to be with my family." He put on his wide-brimmed hat and jumped over the wire fence.

Gyalo, disheartened, looked at the foreigner's back as he was leaving. After the foreigner had walked a few steps, Gyalo shouted in Tibetan, "Hello!" He turned to look at the boy. Gyalo walked to the fence and took out a plastic bag full of yak meat jerky, "Take it, for your trip back." The foreigner seemed to understand what the boy had said. He approached the fence and took the meat. He looked at Gyalo for a moment from behind the brim of his hat and said, "I will come back."

The foreigner turned around and walked a couple more steps but suddenly turned back toward the boy. He took the Potala Palace souvenir badge from his shirt and gave it to Gyalo. The boy hesitated for a moment but took the badge. Delighted, he looked at it carefully. Then, both of them looked at each other without saying a word. The eyes of the foreigner were almost completely covered by his hat. He patted the boy's shoulder and left. His shoes made a lot of noise as he walked.

The sound of his steps could be heard until his silhouette disappeared from the grasslands.

Gyalo, entranced, looked in the direction in which the foreigner had headed until the sound of his steps had completely disappeared. Then Gyalo lifted his head and looked fiercely at the sun. The midday sun was still shining hard on his head. It hurt his eyes badly, but he resisted and did not close them. As the sun blinded him with its myriad of shining white rays, he felt terrified. Gyalo suddenly heard behind him the continuous bleating of lambs.

Wu Yao, *Wish-fulfilling Tree Series, I*

ENTICEMENT

The first time Jamyang Tenzin saw that loose-leaf scripture book tightly wrapped in yellow silk, a profound attraction took hold of him. He was seven years old. That afternoon, he had followed the little girl he'd been playing with to her home through the snow and saw the book lying on the square table in her dark kitchen. Almost everything around it was old: the cupboard, the pots, the bowls, and the dippers blackened with grease. But the book swathed in yellow silk appeared brand-new, and from it there emanated an uncanny golden radiance.

The girl's father was sitting by a low table with his eyes closed, reciting unintelligible six-word mantras that made his lips squirm. Jamyang Tenzin stood dazed, and his eyes began to gleam with a strange, flickering light. Neither the girl nor her father noticed the expression on his face. Suddenly, as if someone had shoved him from behind, he rushed forward, grabbed the book, and started to run out of the house. The girl's father immediately opened his eyes, seized the boy's leg and, with a sudden yank, threw him to the floor. The sacred text fell from Jamyang Tenzin's hands and landed a little way in front of him, still emanating a dazzling golden light. The boy did not cry out or feel any pain. He crawled forward, inching closer to the book. Seeing this, the girl's father stood up and kicked him hard, "You animal! What do you think you're doing?"

Jamyang Tenzin paid no heed, as if he hadn't even heard him, and just kept crawling across the floor. Amazed, the father rushed

Translated from the Chinese by Patricia Schiaffini-Vedani. Originally published in *Literature from Tibet* (*Xizang wenxue*), no. 4 (1995).

forward and picked up the scripture. He turned and stared at the boy in astonishment.

Jamyang Tenzin crept toward the father's feet, grabbed hold of his legs and wouldn't let him walk away. The boy fixed him with a dogged, pleading gaze. The girl's father snapped, "Beast!" Raising the book, he delivered a heavy blow to Jamyang Tenzin's little head. The boy promptly let go, stretched out on the floor with his eyes closed, as if swooned with devotion, and didn't move a muscle. The girl's father demanded she get rid of him at once. Under her father's withering glare, she helped Jamyang Tenzin to his feet and hustled him out of the house.

For a long time after, the spell that the sacred book had cast remained strongly with him.

One day, when he was fifteen years old, he would go to that girl's house and almost marry her. That was three years after her father died. Her name was Rigzin Wangmo.

But even while the father was still alive, Jamyang Tenzin often dropped by for one reason or another, or even for no reason. After the incident with the book, however, Rigzin Wangmo's father began hiding it. Jamyang Tenzin could still sense its presence though. The old fellow had hidden the scripture in a faded and battered trunk that was always secured with a big, rusty lock, but through a crack under the lid, Jamyang Tenzin could make out the glow emanating from the book. When his eyes fixed on that radiance, he became oblivious to his surroundings. Whenever he was absorbed in staring at the old trunk, the girl's father would sneak up and wake him from his reverie with a shove or a kick. With scowls and curses, he would then order his daughter to throw the boy out, making it clear that the boy was never to return. But Jamyang Tenzin would always show up the next day on some pretext. He would search everywhere for the old hidden trunk, falling into a trance when he found it.

One day when he arrived at Rigzin Wangmo's home, he found the door ajar. No one answered when he called. He looked around nervously. Finally, his vision seemed to penetrate the thick walls into a pitch-dark storeroom. In a dusky corner he located the old trunk and, inside it, the sutra tightly wrapped in yellow silk. He stepped quickly to the storeroom door that, at a touch, seemed to open of its own accord. Making his way through the old clothes, he hoisted the trunk onto his back and ran out of the house. The bright noonday sun, hanging in the cloudless sky like a bronze mirror, hurt the eyes. He stopped in the middle of the courtyard and put down the trunk gingerly. A weird light flickered in his eyes, and his pupils grew large. He shook the rusty lock absent-mindedly, and the lock, to his surprise, popped open. Holding his breath, he raised the lid with sudden force. The golden glow from inside the trunk blended into the sunlight. His eyes brimmed over with a kindness and joy he'd never known before. Holding the lid with both hands, he gazed for a long time at the sacred book in ecstasy without daring to touch it. Finally, mustering his courage, he wiped his hands on his clothes, decisively reached in, and took the book out carefully in his right hand. After touching it reverently to his forehead, he put it down to examine it. As he was about to untie the ribbon, the old man appeared in front of him full of wrath. Muttering, the old man grabbed the book by the ribbon and kicked him savagely in the chest. The pages scattered in the air, radiating light, then fell slowly to the ground like snowflakes. At that intensely painful moment, Jamyang Tenzin felt as if he was far away, a silent spectator to this unique event. A knowing smile of happiness crossed his childlike face as he passed out. From that point on, the old man never let him into the house. From dawn to dusk, he stood guard at his door, watching Jamyang Tenzin from a distance with cold, unfathomable eyes. Several times when the old man wasn't around, the boy tried to coax Rigzin Wangmo to let him in to look at the sacred text again, but the girl never relaxed her vigilance and wouldn't let him go where he pleased. Enthralled, he could only gaze with despair, from a distance, at the place that emanated the lovely golden light.

Later, the old man suddenly died, and no one could say what caused his death. It was a chilly afternoon with a blustering wind, and he seemed to sense that he was going to die, for he cracked a bleak smile. From midday on, he insisted that his daughter stay close. At dusk, just as the sun had set behind the mountains and plunged the earth in gloom, the old man expired. His last words were, "You must not let the scriptures fall into that jerk's hands. Someday the rightful owner will come to claim it. He *will* come. On that day you will give it to him." With that, he breathed his last. His face wore a dreadful expression of regret and his eyes stared straight ahead.

After the old man died, Jamyang Tenzin was free to go to the girl's house as often as he liked. However, Rigzin Wangmo vividly remembered her father's cold and forbidding words as well as the terrifying expression on his face when he died, and she was determined not to let Jamyang Tenzin anywhere near the book. More than once, a fantasy came to him of strangling her and absconding with the scriptures to some place far away, but he tried mightily to repress such thoughts.

Day and night, he was often to be seen running to Rigzin Wangmo's home just to gaze at the place that emanated the magnificent golden light.

The year he turned fourteen, she turned sixteen. Each time he asked to see the book, she said he had to marry her first. He never responded to this demand with anything but silence. In his heart, he hated her. The sight of her quivering fleshy cheeks was revolting, and he would often turn away and try to avoid her. At times, she caused him to throw up in his mouth. Whenever he did not comply with her requests, she threw him out of the house, most unpleasantly, and warned him not to come back. The next day, however, he would return as if nothing had happened and pester her to let him see the sutra. She would then express anew her desire to marry him. He would reject her once more, and she would drive him from her house and tell him never to return. Many days went by in this cycle.

One day, during a heavy snowfall, he awoke drowsily at noon and slowly emerged from under his quilt. While he was reluctantly getting dressed, a sudden impulse made him decide to accept Rigzin Wangmo's proposal.

76

He finished dressing and went directly to her house. Pulling her out of bed, he asked to see the book. She rubbed her puffy red eyes, making all the fat on her face jiggle, and burbled, "You want to look at the sutra? Well, then, you have to agree to be my husband."

"I agree," he blurted stiffly.

"Really?" This took her by surprise, but then she sprang to her feet, jubilant. Throwing her arms around his neck, she hugged him and planted crazy kisses all over his face. Although this was extremely painful, he endured it for a while without saying a word. But as her passionate sputters covered his face, he finally couldn't take it any longer and pushed her away.

"OK," he seethed, "Now it's time to bring it out."

Blinking her sunken little eyes and smiling a cunning smile, Rigzin Wangmo demurred, "No, not yet. You have to wait till we're married."

Jamyang Tenzin felt as if someone had taken a bat to his head. He stood there dejected, feeling trapped. Rigzin Wangmo shouldered the faded water cask and went to fetch water. When she came back, he was still standing there, motionless. She put down the cask and came over and tapped him, saying gently, "All right, I'll let you take a quick look." She turned and walked out.

After a little while she came back, shuffling in short quick steps while carefully holding the book in both hands. She stood at some distance and explained gravely, "You can look at it from over there, but you can't get close to it."

His eyes were drawn at once, irresistibly, to the majestic golden light that shone from the sutra. It was just like the first time he had seen it when he was seven years old. In that moment, Jamyang Tenzin felt the rays were aimed at him and were making his head spin, so that it was hard to keep his footing. The silk wrapping looked older than before, but after eight years, the light originating from it was pristine and had retained its true color. Gradually he became aware that the rays from the book were being woven as if by magic into a ceremonial offering scarf of many colors: crimson, orange, yellow, green, blue, and purple. The scarf floated toward him, wound itself around his body, and pulled him steadily toward the sacred scriptures. The girl and everything else vanished from his sight. He could see nothing but the luminous beams from the book, and this taut scarf of many colors reeling him in. With a surging excitement he couldn't explain, he rushed forward and flung himself on the book, meaning to grab it in his arms and run, but just as he turned to flee, he staggered and fell. He couldn't breathe, as if something that weighed a ton, like a boulder, were pressing down on him. Since the sutra was still in his hands, he chose to endure the pain and made no move. Though that boulder-like weight pressed down on his back, there welled up in his heart a sweet joy he had never felt before.

Rigzin Wangmo had stepped forcefully onto his back and was grimacing behind him. She reasoned that as long as she kept him pinned down, even though he had the book, he would not be able to get away. She stayed there a long time and looked quite pleased with herself, so much so that her pudgy face positively quivered. Jamyang Tenzin felt the weight of the boulder on his back getting heavier and heavier. It was hard to breathe, but he endured without a sigh. He didn't try to get up, for he didn't want to risk losing the sutra. But when he couldn't take the pressure any longer, he groaned softly, his forehead beaded in sweat. His heart pounded as if jumping out of his body. Suddenly the heavy burden was lifted off his back. His heart returned to its place, and he exhaled a long breath. Then he heard the distant sound of a woman's voice that was both familiar and unknown, "You still haven't stood up. You're simply insane. Give me back that book right now!"

After lying on the floor a long time, he stood up slowly and then wearily gave Rigzin Wangmo back the sutra. Only then did he realize the strange but familiar voice had come from her mouth. He felt no resentment toward her; on the contrary, he felt she had become more charming and attractive. The boy's deep, melancholy black eyes stared blankly at her for a long time. Seeing this, she became agitated. As far as she could remember, he had never looked at her this way before. She lowered her head, smiling shyly, just glancing at him now and then. The look in his eyes held a touching, true affection, but she slowly became aware that there was something frightening about it too. His eyes aimed straight at her, like two daggers that could pierce the depths of her soul. A wave of fear washed over her and made her shiver. Avoiding his gaze, she raised the scriptures in her hands and whacked Jamyang Tenzin in the head with it three or four times.

"Why are you looking at me like that? It's not like you've never seen me before! We'll soon be husband and wife. You'll be able to feast your eyes on me then. The book will be yours too. Wait for that day!"

He came to his senses as if someone had dumped a bucket of cold water on his head. Flustered, he clapped his hands to his head, nodded to her with an uncertain smile, and ran home. She saw no sign of him for the next seven days.

The evening of the seventh day, Rigzin Wangmo had painstakingly finished the preparations for her wedding. She went to Jamyang Tenzin's house, with nerves aflutter, and found him fast asleep. She became upset, tore off his blanket while muttering curses, and shook him repeatedly, but she couldn't wake him. She took a mouthful of water from the jar and noisily spat it on his face. Jolted awake, he sat up and took a moment to master his confusion. Then he yelled, "I hardly get back from your place and fall asleep and you wake me up. You really are evil!"

"What?" Rigzin Wangmo's eyes opened wide in amazement. "You say you fell asleep after just now getting home?"

"That's right, you horrible woman! Why did you wake me so soon? It's not even dark yet!"

"So you've been sleeping for seven days and seven nights?" Her eyes opened even wider.

"Huh? I slept seven days and seven nights straight? That's impossible. I've been sleeping just a little while." He lay back down, pulled the blanket over his head, and went to sleep again.

After a fortnight, he woke up completely. As soon as he was awake, Rigzin Wangmo hauled him out of bed to get married. It wasn't what you'd call a grand wedding—just the two of them—but it definitely wasn't dreary, either, as she had prepared a lavish banquet and the atmosphere was festive. He didn't know why, but on this occasion the table spread with delicacies made him queasy, and he wanted to vomit. She proposed toast after toast, but he came up with various excuses and let her do the drinking for them both. By the time evening came, Rigzin Wangmo was completely drunk. Her breath reeked of alcohol, and jarring obscenities streamed from her mouth. Jamyang Tenzin was still perfectly sober. Each time she breathed on him, he felt faint and tried to turn away. By the time the sky filled with twinkling stars, they both felt exhausted. Rigzin Wangmo lay down on her brick bed and covered herself with the blanket. Her hand came out from under the quilt and beckoned to him. He didn't want to go to her and remained seated. The image of the sacred book wrapped in yellow silk came to him, and there arose an irresistible yearning to see it right away. With a slightly pleading look in his eyes, he asked, pausing after each word, "So . . . could you let me look at it now?"

Rigzin Wangmo appeared miffed, but only for a moment. She answered in the tone of someone who was managing to control her emotions, "Soon. But you haven't truly become my husband yet. Come. Come now." She lifted a corner of the quilt, once more inviting him to come under the covers. He didn't move, just sat there staring into her face. Since he stayed there like a blockhead, she sat up and began undoing her buttons, taking off her clothes, timidly revealing her naked body. "Come on. Come here. You are my husband now."

Still seated on the edge of her bed, he kept staring at her without moving. Rigzin Wangmo stood up and walked over to him with a swaying gait. She sat in his lap and put her arms around his neck and began planting wild kisses on his face, head, and neck. For some time, he sat there woodenly, but suddenly, he became frightened and started trembling. All he could feel was that the woman who had him in her arms was winding herself round him ever more tightly, like a poisonous snake. With a sudden effort, he pushed her away and glared in rage. "Stop torturing me! Give me the sutra right now!"

When Jamyang Tenzin shoved her away, Rigzin Wangmo's rear end landed on the brick edge of the bed, and she wailed in pain. With a serpentine motion, she crawled back under the quilt and wrapped it tightly round herself. Then she snarled with quivering lips, "You can forget about the book. You'll never touch it again. Go away!!"

He sat there quietly for a long time, regarding her calmly. Then a fit of rage seized him. Trembling all over, he stood up and leaped to grab her by the hair, then knelt on top of her. He took hold of her neck with both hands and began squeezing with all his strength. He kept squeezing. There was a gurgling sound in her throat, and her four limbs danced jerkily in the air like a spider's legs. In the grip of his rage, he kept squeezing her neck, loath to let go. He saw that Rigzin Wangmo was clutching something in her hand and waving it in front of him. He felt a heavy object bounce off his head. Instantly his brain became clouded, and he felt muddled as if he'd entered a thick fog. Relaxing his grip, finally, he stared blankly around the room. At last his gaze took in Rigzin Wangmo's body lying on the brick bed. Although the quilt covered her lower body, her upper body was bare. Her big breasts stood upright like the tops of two hills. An old shoe was tightly gripped in her right hand. She stared at him with eyes round as saucers. He patted her cheek and said, "Hey, Rigzin Wangmo, how can you be like this? Cover yourself with the quilt."

Covering her body, Jamyang Tenzin tried to take the old shoe out of her hand, but he couldn't pry open her fingers, so he put the hand (still holding the shoe) under the cover as well. "That's odd," he muttered, "Why wouldn't you let go of an old shoe?" Then, seeing two deep blood-colored imprints on her neck, he felt something wasn't right. "Are you dead?" he asked, shaking her. "Did somebody kill you?"

Suddenly he noticed bloodstains on his thumbs and forefingers and turned pale. He wept as he studied his hands. "What? These two hands of mine killed her? How can that be? I couldn't kill anyone!"

As he calmed down, he realized that he had indeed killed her, and he rose to his feet uneasily. The more he thought about it, the more frightened he became. He pulled the quilt over her face. If people found out he had killed her, there would be a trial, and he'd have to pay: a life for a life. He began to tremble. Abruptly he lifted her body (still wrapped in the quilt) over his shoulder and carried it out to the door of the storeroom, which he pushed open. He groped his way through the clothes hanging there until he reached that dark corner. Rigzin Wangmo's hand, still clutching the old shoe, came out of the quilt and swayed back and forth in front of his eyes. When he reached the faded trunk, he dropped her body heavily and pushed the trunk to one side, uncovering a dark hole in the floor. He threw her body down the hole and returned the trunk to its original place, covering the hole. The rusty lock with which the trunk was latched made him curious. He examined it quietly, then picked up from a corner of the room a crowbar with which he forced the lock and discarded it. Lifting the lid, he found nothing in the trunk but a sutra wrapped in yellow silk. He leafed through the pages, but finding nothing remarkable in it, he closed the lid and left the house.

Outside, he exhaled a deep breath and ran home. He secured the door of his house from the inside with a thick wooden stake, slipped under his quilt, and fell sound asleep.

He woke up feeling someone patting his face in the darkness. Rigzin Wangmo and her father were standing over him. She was still clutching the old shoe. There was something strange about their bodies, but he couldn't pinpoint what it was. He peered at them groggily and asked, with some irritation, "Why did you wake me up? I want to sleep!"

Rigzin Wangmo's father looked grave as he hauled Jamyang Tenzin out of bed, but his voice was gentle. "You disturbed my sutra. You were the only one who knew where it was hidden. You can't stay here now. Come along." He took him by the hand. Jamyang Tenzin thought about shaking him off and returning to the warmth and comfort of his bed, but looking at the old man's grim face, he felt scared. He followed them out of the house reluctantly. On the road, he saw the stars gradually disappearing. Just before dawn, a meteor slipped rapidly toward the horizon and was gone in a flash.

By noon the sky was swirling with snowflakes. A party of Buddhist monks on horseback sped toward Jamyang Tenzin's home with a throng hurrying behind them. They dismounted a few dozen paces from his house and continued on foot, followed by the crowd of villagers who were gabbling about something in low voices. They all stopped in front of his door. In this group there was a monk rather advanced in years who stepped up to the door, took hold of the knocker, and began rapping gently. Though he kept knocking for a long time, no one came to open the door. The villagers watched him and didn't utter a word. The old monk's fingers grew numb from knocking, so he let go of the ring and tried pushing. The door didn't budge, as it was locked from the inside. Without any haste, he turned to call a young monk over and, leaning close to his ear, quietly gave him instructions. In a few strides, the young monk climbed the elm planted beside the door and let himself down into the courtyard from the top of the wall. Monks and villagers watched the door, waiting for something to happen. All of a sudden, the door clanked open. All eyes locked on the young monk as he appeared in the doorway. With a mournful countenance, he scurried to the old monk and whispered breathlessly in a voice that sounded like the noise of an insect, "The Buddha has passed away!"

Though his voice was low, everyone heard him. The humming sound that had issued from the young monk's mouth was a bolt from the blue that left them all wide-eyed and dumbstruck with horror. The old monk was the first to recover. With a grave face, he called a few young monks over and quietly gave instructions. They then entered Jamyang Tenzin's house together. The crowd that had followed along became upset; the women lowered their heads and wept while the men, too, showed signs of grief.

The old men who had known Jamyang Tenzin very well sat down in a group and reminisced with many a sigh. A little old man with a lined face stroked his goatee and spoke slowly to the old fellows gathered round, "We're a bunch of dummies not to have recognized a true Buddha in our midst. Remember, guys? They say that on the day the Buddha was born, the dry pear tree by the river produced a blossom—and you know that was in winter; it was snowing!" Dropping his old face, as dry as a walnut, into his big coarse hands, another old man murmured in confession, "This is my sin: that year the young Buddha came to my yard to steal pears.... No, no, *no*! Can you believe what just came out of my rotten mouth? What I mean is, that year when the young Buddha came to pick pears, I spanked him without mercy. Yes, a grievous sin.... Come to think of it, I've heard that on the day the Holy One was born, an auspicious light appeared in the eastern sky for several minutes. We didn't know then what it meant."

The young monks who had gone into the house did not emerge, so the villagers continued their discussions outside.

Jamyang Tenzin was being guided by Rigzin Wangmo and her father to a place he'd never seen before. It was barren all around; nothing grew there. They were walking at the bottom of a long and narrow gorge.

An old man with white hair and a wan complexion appeared in front of them. He stepped up to Jamyang Tenzin and grabbed his hand, "Why are you here, Son?" Jamyang Tenzin shook his head in puzzlement. At that moment, Rigzin Wangmo's father, still holding her hand, knelt before the old man and cried, "He found the sacred book and touched it. I could not be at ease, so I brought him here."

The gray-haired old man looked at Rigzin Wangmo and her father and exploded, "You animals! The Buddha is right in front of you, and you don't kneel to him. The rightful owner of the sutra, which I entrusted to you years ago, is the Living Buddha Jamyang Tenzin." He turned to Jamyang Tenzin with a kindly smile.

Rigzin Wangmo and her father panicked. Still on their knees, they shuffled toward Jamyang Tenzin to embrace his legs and lick his shoes as they implored, "Holiness, please forgive us. We were too ignorant to recognize a true Buddha." Jamyang Tenzin felt increasingly confused. He had no idea what they were talking about, so he kicked them away.

The gray-haired old man caressed Jamyang Tenzin's face with his big, cold hand. "Son, go back. The people there are waiting. They need you. In five years, we'll meet here again." Indicating the direction he had to take, he urged him to leave. After a few steps, Jamyang Tenzin looked back and saw the old man leading Rigzin Wangmo and her father in the opposite direction.

Jamyang Tenzin heard the sound of drums and cymbals and readings from the scriptures calling to him from far away. He slowly opened his eyes and, rubbing them vigorously, found himself surrounded by a throng of loudly chanting monks in burgundy robes. He gaped at them. "What are you all doing here?"

Hearing a voice coming from who knows where, the monks stopped their chant and glanced around, perplexed, until they noticed that Jamyang Tenzin was slowly rising from his bed.

"The Living Buddha has come back to life!" they yelled, their faces beaming with joy.

"What? Back to life? Was I dead?" Jamyang Tenzin looked alarmed. A short old monk approached, head down, palms together in front of his chest as he bowed in salutation. "Your Holiness did not abandon all living things in this abyss of worldly suffering to go to the Land of Bliss. Wise indeed is the Buddha!"

When the short old monk raised his head, Jamyang Tenzin peered at him anxiously. He wiped his eyes in disbelief and looked at him again. The old monk was none other than Rigzin Wangmo's late father! He almost blurted, "Hey, old fellow, weren't you dead? How come you're still here?" but he held his tongue. It was amusing to watch the old man fussing with his robes.

The rituals continued the next day with great fanfare. Then everyone left except the short old monk, who stayed to wait upon Jamyang Tenzin's every need.

Early the next morning, right after sunrise, a crowd of pious Buddhist laypeople gathered at Jamyang Tenzin's door. They chose one of them to negotiate with the old monk for an audience with the Buddha. After the old monk had talked to Jamyang Tenzin privately for quite some time, they were allowed to enter. The villagers formed a long winding line like a dragon. They drew near and bowed to him with ceremonial silk scarves in their hands, then made their offerings, performed full-body prostrations, and let the Buddha touch their heads. Stealing glances up at Jamyang Tenzin, they showed their tongues in respect, swallowed two mouthfuls of saliva, and quickly stepped back. Then, one by one, they departed.

When Jamyang Tenzin was finally about to return to his room to rest, he saw a woman approaching who held in her outstretched hands a book wrapped in yellow silk. He thought she looked familiar. With eyes averted, she knelt down and lifted the sutra above her head in offering. As soon as he held the book in his hands, he beheld a myriad of golden rays shining upon him. He suddenly remembered what had happened when he was seven years old, and he embraced the sutra, murmuring something under his breath. When the prostrate woman turned her face to him, he recognized her as Rigzin Wagmo, who had wanted to make him her husband. He instinctively recoiled as a strange dread came over him. He clutched the scriptures more tightly and shouted, "I won't be your husband, I won't! I want this book. *I want this book!*"

Hearing the shouting, the little old monk and the others gathered round in curiosity. They touched him reassuringly and asked, "What's the matter? What happened?"

Shaking with fear, Jamyang Tenzin jabbed a finger toward Rigzin Wangmo and bellowed, "I won't be her husband. *I will not be her husband!*"

Perplexed, the monks turned to Rigzin Wangmo. She paled and prostrated, trembling as she repeated, "Calm yourself, calm yourself, your Holiness. I am a sinful woman and I shouldn't have come here. I just wanted to give you the sutra that ought to have been yours long ago."

It came back to him then that the old gray-haired man had said something along those lines. But as he recalled the old man's saying they would meet again in five years, a jolt of terror shot through him.

Mastering his fear, he clapped his hands, signaling Rigzin Wangmo to leave. The little old monk, still bowed, quietly approached and took the scriptures from his arms.

"Your Holiness cannot yet open this sutra. It will completely belong to Your Holiness on his twentieth birthday," he said calmly. "At that time I will bring it back for you to open it yourself." That said, the monk took it away and put it in a brand-new trunk, which he locked.

The next day, several young monks came with a horse to fetch Jamyang Tenzin. They took him to a monastery where he began learning how to read and how to recite passages from Buddhist texts. The short old monk was his preceptor, and a very strict one too. The first thing the monk did, with the aid of a ladder, was to hide the trunk underneath a statue of the Buddha in a place Jamyang Tenzin couldn't reach. Every day, the old monk made him light a butter lamp in front of it and prostrate three times. On each occasion, he could see golden rays shining out from this place. The beams of light made him feel dizzy, as if in love. Though he longed to get his hands on the sutra, it was too high. Besides, the old monk was watching him like a hawk.

Whenever the golden rays stirred in him those feelings of vertigo and enticement, he'd be overcome by an urge to see the sacred book. He would beg then, but the old monk always shook his head in refusal.

When he turned seventeen, Jamyang Tenzin beseeched the monk, "Only three more years to go! Come on, bring it down and let me take a look."

The little old monk looked somewhat alarmed but replied with composure, "Holy One, you mustn't say things like that. You will cause us much pain, we who are immersed in this sea of suffering. The sutra will of course become yours when you turn twenty."

When he turned eighteen, Jamyang Tenzin beseeched the monk, "Only two more years to go! Come on, bring it down and let me take a look."

The little old monk looked somewhat alarmed but, again, replied with composure, "Holy One, you mustn't say things like that. You will cause us much pain, we who are immersed in this sea of suffering. The sutra will of course become yours when you turn twenty."

When he turned nineteen, Jamyang Tenzin beseeched the monk, "Only one more year to go! Come on, bring it down and let me take a look."

The little old monk looked somewhat alarmed but, again, replied with composure, "Holy One, you mustn't say things like that. You will cause us much pain, we who are immersed in this sea of suffering. The sutra will of course become yours when you turn twenty."

It was a cold winter morning when Jamyang Tenzin turned twenty years old. The little old monk brought down from underneath the Buddha-statue that sacred book tightly wrapped in yellow silk and came into the room ready to present it to Jamyang Tenzin. He found him sitting upright in the lotus position, eyes closed and palms joined. The old monk stood respectfully to one side and called softly to him, but there was no response. Then he lightly touched Jamyang Tenzin's knee, again without response. He was beginning to get nervous. He knelt down and took hold of Jamyang Tenzin's hand, feeling for a pulse, but found his pulse had ceased to beat. Deeply shocked, he cried in bitter grief, "O Sacred Buddha! So you were, indeed, the divinity foretold. Woe to us sinners, ignorant as dirt! We couldn't let you have in this life what you longed for. I bring it to you now that it is yours. Gaze on it to your heart's content!"

And with that, the old monk untied the ribbon and opened the scriptures to the first page, gently placing it in Jamyang Tenzin's lap.

Jamyang Tenzin found himself floating on air. When he saw the silk-encased book finally open on his lap, there welled up in his heart a sweetness and joy he had not felt for many years. After the monks had carried out for forty-nine days the funeral rites of the Bardo, Jamyang Tenzin's body—still sitting in the lotus position, with eyes closed and palms joined—was placed, together with that sacred sutra wrapped round in yellow silk, inside a small stupa filled with cedar branches, and this was set ablaze.

As the raging fire burned higher, the monks knelt with bowed heads and noiselessly recited the *Sutra on Passing from One Existence to Another*. A young monk could not help raising his head to peek. He beheld Jamyang Tenzin, the Living Buddha, holding in both hands the sacred book wrapped in yellow silk. He floated into the heavens along a radiant path of light, and then was gone.

A NEW GOLDEN CORPSE TALE: GUN

When Decho Zangpo rushed back to the cemetery of Dewatsal, corpses big and small begged him, "Take me, take me, please!" Decho Zangpo recited a prayer several times, and the corpses fell one after another. He proceeded further and saw that the Golden Corpse* *had climbed up a sandalwood tree. He was pleading, "Don't take me, please!" He glared at the Golden Corpse and said, holding the crescent moon-shaped ax as he was ready to cut down the tree, "I am Decho Zangpo. Nāgārjuna*[†] *is my Master, the ax is my tool, the leather bag is for you, and the rope is to tie you up. You, listen up! Are you coming down, or do I have to cut down the tree?"*

Upon hearing that, the Golden Corpse, trembling, climbed down from the tree. Timidly looking at Decho Zangpo and turning himself over, he entered the leather bag. Decho Zangpo, relieved, kicked the Golden Corpse before tightly closing the bag with the rope. He was thinking, "You, damn Corpse

---

Translated from the Chinese by Patricia Schiaffini-Vedani. Originally published in *Literature from Tibet* (*Xizang wenxue*), no. 1 (1997).

*   *Tales of the Golden Corpse* (*Mi ro gser sgrung*) is a collection of traditional Tibetan folk tales. Similar stories of a magical talking corpse can be found in other areas in South Asia and Inner Asia. Pema Tseden, as most Tibetans, grew up listening to relatives and neighbors telling these stories that, for generations, were narrated both to entertain and to teach moral principles. Although not written this way in the original Chinese story, the translator has chosen to write in italics the part of the story corresponding to the traditional tale, and in roman font the additions made by Pema Tseden.

†   Nāgārjuna was an Indian Buddhist philosopher who lived in the 2nd century CE.

have caused all this trouble. I have come a long way to get you. This time I am definitely going to bring you to Master Nāgārjuna to fulfill my promise!"

Decho Zangpo took a ball of butter and roasted barley flour that Master Nāgārjuna had given him and, shouldering the Golden Corpse, headed back to the road.

After a while the Golden Corpse asked, "Hey, brother, to shorten the trip we need a strong horse, but neither of us has one, so we will have to talk away the trip. We can both do this! Why don't you tell me a story? Or I can tell you one."

Decho Zangpo heard the Golden Corpse but remembered what Master Nāgārjuna had told him, so he ignored him and kept going.

Decho Zangpo used to be called Dhondup, but Master Nāgārjuna gave him this new name. When he was called Dhondup, his older brother, Salche, went to study magic with the famous Seven Warlock Brothers in the hope of bringing a better life to both of them. Salche thought that it would be very nice if he could learn from the seven famed magicians some tricks like turning things into butter or roasted barley flour. He spent three years with them, but whenever they were practicing magic, they would send him to work far away, so he could not observe them. Even though Salche had barely enough food or clothing to get by, he forced himself to stay there.

One day, his brother Dhondup came by to bring him food and stayed with him overnight. That night, Dhondup, who was smart and careful, quietly approached the seven brothers' residence and found them practicing magic. He saw all the spells they were practicing from beginning to end and, without forgetting anything, he mastered all their magical secrets. After that, he went back to Salche's place and woke him up, saying, "Brother, if you stay here you may never learn magic after all. What is the point in so much work and suffering? Let's go home!" Salche agreed and returned home with Dhondup that same night.

When they got home, Dhondup said, "Brother, we have a white horse at our stable. Don't take it anywhere near the seven warlocks' place. Go somewhere else to sell it, so you can use the money to buy things you can bring back home." After saying this, he immediately ran to the stable and turned himself into a white horse. When Salche went to the stable, he sure enough found an extraordinary steed. Joyful, Salche completely forgot his brother's warnings. Smiling with pride, he thought that his brother was very smart. He had not learned any magic during the three years he spent with the seven brothers, but his brother had gotten this fine horse! For a long time, he thought about whether he should sell the horse or keep it as his own mount.

Early the next morning, the seven brothers went to Salche's place only to find it empty. Cunning and cruel by nature, the warlock brothers said, "The two brothers left! They must have secretly learned something from us when we were carelessly practicing magic last night."

The older brother noted, "As the saying goes, while the reins of a horse should be long, the ax that cuts the tree should be sharp. We cannot let these two brothers go so lightly. The vast grassland can be destroyed by a tiny spark of fire, and an ant hole can cause a great dike to collapse. If we don't eliminate these two, there will be no end to our troubles. They will damage our reputation."

The seven warlocks transformed themselves into seven wealthy merchants, and with mules laden with goods, they hurried to where Dhondup and his brother lived. Although the meaning of Salche's name was intelligent, he was in fact a bit naïve, so he did not realize that the seven merchants were in fact the seven warlocks in disguise. He brought them into his house and offered them his hospitality, thinking, "That common saying is right: good luck comes to good people. This opportunity of business came so unexpectedly to my door!" When the warlocks saw the white steed tied up to the stake, they knew it had to be the product of magic. They bargained with Salche for a while and finally left with the horse, paying one hundred gold liang.

Pulling the horse, the warlock brothers laughed and said, "In a little while, let's kill this horse. Let's dismember it in ten thousand pieces!" Although Dhondup, in the shape of that horse, was unable to talk, deep inside he was certain of what was going to happen and feared for his life. When the warlocks arrived at the marshes of a small river, the sixth of the brothers erected a stove to boil water while the youngest stood there holding the horse. Dhondup was scared—his heart pounded loudly. When he saw that the brother holding him was not paying attention, he struggled free of the reins and ran away. The brothers chased after him, shouting madly that they would kill him. But right when they were about to nab him, the horse saw a fish swimming in the river, changed into a fish himself, and swam to the center of the stream. The seven brothers immediately turned into seven otters and swam after him. Seeing he was about to be caught, the fish saw a dove flying in the sky, shook his body once to become a dove, and flew into the sky flapping his wings. The seven warlocks soon transformed themselves into seven hawks and continued the chase. Desperately, the white dove flew to take refuge in a mountain cave.

Inside the cave, master Nāgārjuna was meditating. Upon entering the cave, the dove recovered his original human appearance and respectfully greeted the master, saying, "As the saying goes, you report good news to the officials, but you only share the bad news with your master; you provide food for your parents, but you only tell the truth to your master. I am being chased by the seven warlock brothers. I have no one to rely on. I implore you, great master ... save me!"

The master, who was merciful to every living being, felt compassion for this youngster. "What is the need of seeking enlightenment if one does not pity and rescue those in need? I do not concern myself with everyday affairs, but your situation is critical. Besides, seven people harassing one is against the essence of Buddhism and against conventional wisdom. Why don't you become one of the prayer beads in my hand?" Dhondup changed his shape into a bead and rested safely under the master's thumb.

In no time, the seven warlocks entered the cave and assumed the form of seven commoners. They addressed the master saying, "Hey, old man, where is that white dove that entered the cave not long ago? Give it to us at once!" The master, eyes closed, continued reciting the Om mantra and did not respond. Seeing this, the seven brothers howled at him, "Are you deaf or what? Are you going to surrender the dove? If not, don't blame us for what we will do to you." The seven brothers changed shape into seven centipedes and climbed up the master's body.

Dhondup became very worried. "What if they harm the master because of me? What should I do?" Then he transformed himself into a rooster and one by one pecked the seven centipedes to death. Immediately the centipedes became human corpses.

Disturbed by what he had seen, master Nāgārjuna said, "Oh, seven lives taken, such a great sin!"

Dhondup, distressed, replied, "Master, you saved my life. To repair this great sin and repay your benevolence, I will remain at your service for anything you need me to do."

Seeing his remorse, the master tried to comfort him, "Don't agonize over this. What has happened cannot be changed, so there is no use in regret. But you will have to make amends for what you have done."

"How can I make up for this?" asked Dhondup.

"You'll head west, crossing many mountains, until you reach a place called Dewatsal cemetery. There you will find the Golden Corpse of Good Fortune. It is a treasure from head to toe; its upper body is made of jade, and its lower body is made of gold. He can make common people live long and plentiful lives. If you obtain the Golden Corpse, your sin will disappear."

"That is easy to do," answered Dhondup.

Master Nāgārjuna replied, "It will not be an easy task. It is not as simple as carrying something on your back. Remember that you should shut your mouth and not say a word while you are carrying it home. If you talk, all will be lost."

Dhondup vowed to bring the Golden Corpse back, so as to provide happiness to people and to eliminate his own sin. Before leaving, the master advised, "When you get to the cemetery, many corpses of all sizes will implore you to take them. Recite a spell and all of them but one will fall down. Those who fall are not the ones you are looking for. But there will be one still standing who will climb to a sandalwood tree and say to you 'Don't take me, don't take me.' That is the Golden Corpse of Good Fortune you'll have to bring back. When you take the ax and pretend you are going to cut the tree, the Golden Corpse will quickly come down. Load it in this leather bag that can hold all living things and tie the bag tightly with this rope. On the way back, eat these balls of roasted barley flour and butter, walk day and night and don't say a word. You must remember this: if you talk, the Golden Corpse will fly back to the Dewatsal cemetery.

"Since destiny brought you to this cave of Decho, I will give you the Buddhist name of Decho Zangpo." This said, the master gave him the tools he would need in his journey.

At the request of master Nāgārjuna, Decho Zangpo headed west, surmounting a journey of untold dangers and difficulties in order to retrieve the Golden Corpse. However, every time he got the Golden Corpse and headed back, the body would fascinate Decho Zangpo with his stories and lure him into speaking, which resulted in the Golden Corpse fleeing, and Decho Zangpo wasting precious time and effort. The last time this happened was when the Golden Corpse told the story, "The Lion Statue Opens its Mouth." The story made Decho Zangpo feel that justice had been served, so without noticing it, he cried out loud, "Such a greedy guy, he deserved it!" which allowed the Golden Corpse to return to the Dewatsal Cemetery once more.

Now as they set off once more, the Golden Corpse, seeing that Decho Zangpo was not paying attention to him, said, "Oh, since you don't want to talk, let me tell you a story." Decho Zangpo, with his heart in his mouth, lowered his head and tried to ignore him. "Before, I always told you stories that happened long, long ago, but now I will tell you a story that will happen in the future, some time from now."

Upon hearing this, Decho Zangpo was a bit perplexed. "How can this sly corpse know what is going to happen in the future?"

The Golden Corpse continued his story. "Sometime in the future, there will be a youngster called Mingme, which in fact means 'without name.' His parents will have three kids, one after another, but none of them will live. After Mingme's birth, in order to avoid the fate of the other babies who would die prematurely, his parents will ask the lama at his village to find a name for him. This will be the name chosen for him in order to keep him safe.

"Born into the most affluent family in the village, and being the only child, Mingme will be extremely spoiled. Relying on his family's money, Mingme will do as he pleases, acting like a despot and building for himself a terrible reputation among the villagers. From a young age, gambling and hunting will be his favorite past times. With the former, he will squander his family's money, and with the latter, he will amuse himself. At age fifteen, as a result of his gambling with the other rich kids from the village, he will have already lost half of his family's wealth. Their way of gambling will be very particular. They will ignite a fire with mulberry branches on the stage at the center of the village and blow the conch-shell trumpet.* The one able to make the sound of the conch shell last the longest will be the winner. This way of gambling will elicit critiques from some elders in the village, who will see this as an insult to the deities, but the youngsters will not be dissuaded. This kind of competition will often leave Mingme in a terrible physical condition, because being so fat and out of shape, even a simple walk will make him gasp for breath. It will not bother him to lose money this way though. On the contrary, losing will make him participate in the competitions with even more interest. Often, after the mulberry burns to ashes and the white conch trumpet determines the winner, this rich boy, full of zest, will go hunting.

"On both sides of the village there will be two high mountains with plenty of cypress trees and many kinds of shrubs at their feet. The many hunters in the village will hunt to their hearts' content in these areas, which will be inhabited by mountain goats, foxes, rabbits, and other animals. Behind the village there will be a lower mountain that, according to legend, is sacred. On its top will live a dozen or so musk deer said to be the livestock of the mountain god. Needless to say, nobody will dare hunt them. These rich kids and the other hunters will go back home carrying rabbits and other prey under the gaze of the sacred mountain's musk deer, who will graze there at their leisure. The rich kids will all have

---

* The white conch is used as a trumpet in Buddhist ceremonies, symbolizing the sound of Buddhism. It is one of the Eight Auspicious Symbols of Buddhism.

guns, which will make hunting very efficient. Once hit by a bullet, it will be very difficult for an animal to escape death.

"Brother Decho Zangpo, do you know what a gun is?"

At this point, the Golden Corpse stopped his story and asked the question again, trying to elicit a verbal response from Decho Zangpo. Decho Zangpo, who was still clear headed, secretly cursed him, "You, damned corpse!" He looked back at the Golden Corpse resolutely and thought, "Who cares what that thing is? I will not be fooled again so easily!"

The Golden Corpse waited in silence, hoping that the climax of his story would make Decho Zangpo speak. Decho Zangpo looked back again in anger and, using his elbow, ruthlessly hit the bag containing the Golden Corpse as he continued walking ahead. Realizing that Decho Zangpo had not fallen into his trap, the Golden Corpse continued telling the story.

"By Mingme's nineteenth birthday there will not be much left of his family's fortune. His parents' hair will have turned white worrying about their useless son and, in vain, trying to prevent him from gambling. Around this time, a long-time friend of his father will bring his own daughter and say, 'My dear friend, I truly cannot bear to see how your son continues ruining your family's fortune. Without any requests, I bring my own beloved daughter to marry your son. Maybe once he settles down and marries, he will look ahead.'

"The old couple, not knowing what to do, will shed tears of gratitude. After the friend leaves, they will call their son back home to tell him, 'We want you to marry her. From now on you will conduct yourself properly.'

"Seeing her appearance, Mingme will happily agree to the marriage. But when the old parents look for the only sage nearby to choose an auspicious day for the wedding, the sage will calmly tell them, 'Even if you find him ten wives, he will still not change his faulty ways. Sooner or later, he will not only wither away your family's fortune, but will destroy himself as well. But you still depend on him to carry on your ancestral line.' Scared, the parents will choose a date for their son's wedding.

"Nyima Lhamo, Mingme's wife, will be beautiful, kindhearted, and gentle. She will try to move her husband with her gentle and honest ways so as to change his conduct and deeds. However, all her efforts will fail. Her innate goodness and endless tenderness will not change her husband's vile nature. His interest in her beauty and her body will last only a short while. After a month or so, he will start to show that he is weary of her. But in this short period of happiness, he will sow his seed in her, even though he will still be unable to free himself from the pleasure of gambling. After marrying, he will gain even more weight, so his greater lack of fitness will make him lose even more money. At the age of twenty, he will have ruined her family's entire fortune. This same year, Nyima Lhamo will give him a son. The grandparents will not ask a lama to name the child this time. They will name him themselves: Lengan, meaning 'the unfortunate.'

"Once their son has a son who can continue the ancestral line, the old couple will find themselves irremediably immersed in a myriad of contradictory feelings. They will feel at the same time happy and sad, relieved and worried. But not too long after this, they will both pass away. Just as the birth of his son will not elicit many feelings in Mingme, the death of his parents will not give him much distress.

"Around that time, Mingme will sell his ancestors' home, the oldest house in the village, to continue gambling. But as one can imagine, he will not win any money and instead will lose everything. Seeing that he has nothing left, those gambling friends who used to call him brother will begin to ignore him, not letting him into their gambling parties. Kneeling in front of his gambling friends, he will beg them to let him gamble one last time. Seeing him begging so pathetically, one of them will say with contempt, 'Okay. If you win this one, we will give you the house back; but if you lose, what will you give us as collateral?'

"Stunned by their answer, he will stay there for a long time, speechless and embarrassed. After a long while, the image of his wife and son will emerge in front of his eyes. With some excitement, and without thinking twice, he will say, 'I put forward my wife and son as collateral.'

"Upon hearing this, the gamblers will laugh and say, 'Your wife is still good looking, she is barely passable as collateral. But your son. . . . If we win him, he will just be a burden. . . . Forget about him.' This said, they will start their special game.

"After burning the mulberry branches and saying some prayers, Mingme and two other rich youngsters will begin to blow the conchshell trumpets. This time, using his full strength, Mingme will be able to blow the trumpet for half an hour—his face and neck swollen and red; his cheeks bulging and sticking out as if about to burst; his eyes wide open and teary. The other two rich fellows will also exert all their strength—their red necks and faces and their protruding cheeks and eyes will look quite scary. Finally, Mingme will be the one who, unable to stand it any longer, stops first. Upon stopping, he will fall to the ground unconscious. A few seconds later, the other two will fall unconscious as well.

"So this is how Mingme's wife, Nyima Lhamo, and their child will be taken away by his gambling friends. At that moment, Mingme's heart will experience a sense of loss; his usual feelings of not caring about anything he has when he is not gambling will now be gone. Afterwards, that sense of loss will give way to an indescribable feeling of wrath. He will look around and angrily pick up his gun from the ground. That will be his sole possession. Besides it, he will have nothing.

"But his ire will not make him use the gun to bring back the wife and child that were taken away from him. Instead, he will take the gun to the mountains to hunt. He will want to hunt as a way to wash away the unspeakable anger. Heading to the sacred mountains behind the village, he will see several musk deer grazing leisurely at the foot of the mountains. Suddenly, it will occur to him that musk is very expensive and could sell for a high price, so he will change course and walk to the foot of the mountain. Even though he will approach very close, the musk deer will continue grazing without lifting their heads. He will remember that the musk deer belong to the mountain deity; nobody in the village would dare think of killing them. The elders would say that whoever had the bad idea of harming these musk deer would be in big trouble. Mingme will feel worried, and even a bit scared, so he will stop, not daring to approach them. He will have conflicting feelings, will be unable to decide whether or not to do it. A voice in his ear will whisper softly, 'Go for it, go for it! If you kill one musk deer you will get a lot of money—your chance to win it all back!' But after this voice stops, another voice will severely warn him, 'Put down your weapon and stop walking forward. If you dare touch a single hair of the mountain god's livestock, you will not even have time to regret it!' Faced with this dilemma, he will stand in the grass without moving.

"At that moment, one of the musk deer grazing ahead will lift its head to look at Mingme and slowly start to walk in Mingme's direction. Mingme will hear again the two voices speaking one after another in his ears, to the point that he will not be able to ignore them. In the end, the first voice will impose itself, controlling him completely. Looking at the musk deer approaching, he will drop to the ground, softly raising his gun to aim carefully. But in the moment he aims at the musk deer, his eyes will see three visions, one after another: first, the face of an old man, his head completely covered in white hair; second, the face of a ferocious-looking woman; and finally, a half-human-half-beast monster. His forehead will start to seep fine beads of sweat that will slowly fall down into his eyes, clouding his vision. The sweat will make his palms so wet that he will not be able to grasp his weapon firmly. These three visions will last several minutes. Although he will want to take back the original thought of killing the musk deer, his finger will involuntarily pull the trigger. The muffled sound of the gunshot will proclaim that all has ended. The musk deer grazing nearby will flee in all directions. Mingme will lie on the ground. From his forehead, a black hole the size of a gun muzzle will pour blood."

The Golden Corpse stopped his story. Leaning over Decho Zangpo's back, he waited for Decho Zangpo to talk. Decho Zangpo had indeed submerged himself in the story's tragic setting, and he was completely subdued by this tale. There was a question he wanted to blurt out, "Who shot Mingme in the forehead?" However, he realized he was slowly entering the trap that the Golden Corpse had long ago set up for him. Secretly glad he had not uttered the question out loud, he waited for the Golden Corpse to continue telling the story so as to solve the puzzle. As if he had guessed Decho Zangpo's thoughts, the Golden Corpse sealed his mouth and did not say a word.

There was a short period of silence between them, and Decho Zangpo's mind could not help but drift to other thoughts. He thought of his simple and honest elder brother, Salche. A bit worried, he wondered, "Is my brother alright now? Alone, he should be able to barely make a living." After that he complained to himself a bit, "Brother, had you not sold me to the seven warlocks, I would not be enduring this suffering now. And we, brothers, would not have been separated...."

Interrupting his thought, the Golden Corpse resumed his story. "The news that Mingme died violently because he tried to kill the sacred mountain's musk deer will spread all over, like the wind. After people debate the news for a while, they will come to this conclusion: those who host improper thoughts about the musk deer of the sacred mountain will attract upon themselves the misfortune of murder.

"After Mingme's death, the gamblers will set Nyima Lhamo and her son free. For her and her son, it will be a life of solitude and hardship in which living through one day will seem like surviving a whole year. Under Nyima Lhamo's painstaking care, and surrounded by difficulty and misery, little Lengan will gradually grow up to become a graceful youngster. Nyima Lhamo will have hoped that Lengan, upon growing up, might share with her the responsibilities of life. However, contrary to his mother's expectations, at a young age Lengan will develop a keen interest in gambling. He will often gather a group of companions to play gambling games in which he can win some food and things like that. Nyima Lhamo will sigh in despair, all day thinking to herself that this is the sin of her gambling-addict late husband. But as it pertains to gambling, Lengan will not be like his father, who only knew how to lose. Among the young gamblers, Lengan will rarely lose. But Nyima Lhamo will not be at all happy about the odd things he will win; in fact, it will cause her extreme restlessness and panic.

"Lengan's way of gambling will be entirely new, nothing like the ways of the previous generations in which winning or losing was based on blowing the conch shell trumpets. They will play a wonderful game of cards, one that Lengan will master almost to perfection. When completely concentrating on the game, Lengan will forget about everything else; he will play recklessly for three days and nights without sleep and without feeling tired. If winning the game, he will completely forget about his mother.

"Due to excessive hardships, Nyima Lhamo's body will be plagued with serious illnesses that will often keep her bedridden. His mind lost in gambling and too busy to take care of anything else, Lengan will ignore his mother's poor health. Whenever disease will torment her to the point of not letting her walk, a stream of grief will rush through her heart. Beside herself, she will cry uncontrollably. Then she will feel there is no one on earth as unfortunate as she. This will increase her grief and will make her cry even louder, making all neighbors around sigh and take pity on her.

"Nyima Lhamo will try time and time again to calmly convince and teach Lengan, but he will always turn a deaf ear; sometimes he will even fiercely refute her. Feeling helpless, she will go see the village sage to tell her of her son's fortune. The sage will close his eyes in contemplation for a while, and slowly open his mouth to tell her, 'For some time it will be very hard for this son of yours to regain control of his mind, but when a black mole appears in the center of his forehead, he will come to his senses. Then he will become a filial son like no other.'

"Upon hearing the words of the sage, Nyima Lhamo will become very happy, her heart full of hope. She will go back home and always observe her son, waiting to see a black mole miraculously appear on his bright and clear forehead. But one year, two years, three years will pass by, and the black mole she so longs for will not appear. Contrary to her expectations, his gambling will get even worse, and he will show no indication of coming to his senses. Afterwards, her condition will worsen to the point of almost not being able to move.

"With the New Year approaching, the village will suddenly become freezing cold. A spell of gloomy and gelid north wind will come down and sweep past the village, causing the will of the people to drain away. Sick in bed, Nyima Lhamo will hope for her son to come back for the preparations of the New Year's celebration, but her son will have been absent already for three days and nights.

"On the last day of the lunar year, Lengan will be sitting with some young guys on an empty piece of land, playing his gambling game of cards. When darkness falls upon them on New Year's Eve, they will have no intention of going back home. One of them will steal a paper lantern and, under its flickering light, lost in themselves, they will play cards and gamble. Their faces will be white and their lips cracked, but in their eyes will shine a strange light of excitement. Sometimes the roaring, chilly north wind will roil up the dust and throw it on their heads. They will ignore it after spitting a couple of times.

"When the curtain of light completely falls, one of the gamblers, under the flickering lantern, will point to Lengan's face in amazement, saying, 'You've got a black mole on your forehead!' Clicking their tongues in wonder, the rest will also look at his forehead. At that moment, Lengan will feel an indescribable change in his body. It will look as if he is about to faint. He will throw away the cards in his hands and stand up. Gradually, he will think about his bedridden mother and will leave everything behind to run back home.

"Once he gets home and sees his mother so extremely thin and pallid, he will feel very sad and will start to cry. 'Mother, I have failed you. From today on, I will take care of you!' he will shout loudly while crying. His mother will stare in disbelief at her son's face while trying to raise her body from the bed. But seeing the black mole on his forehead, a smile will gradually appear on her face. Putting her palms together in prayer, she will recite the name of the sage.

"After he regains control of himself, Lengan will carry his mother on his back and rush to see the village doctor. The doctor's family, already done with the New Year's Eve's dinner and getting ready to sleep, will be very surprised to see Lengan, such an uncaring son, carrying his mother upon his back. Lengan will humbly ask the doctor to treat his mother's illness, but the doctor, seeing the strange mole on his forehead, will ask perplexed, 'When did you get that black mole on your forehead?' The doctor's family will echo his surprise with similar exclamations. After that, the doctor will take Nyima Lhamo's pulse and, looking somber, will tell Lengan, 'Your mother's body is contaminated by multiple illnesses. It will require a long healing process. In order to make her medicine I will need musk as a starter. At the moment, I do not have musk. If you can find some, then I can make the medicine and start the treatment.'

"This will cause Lengan to sink into a state of desperation. He will think, 'I am a penniless good-for-nothing. Where will I ever find that precious musk?' On the way back, it will be impossible for him to find peace of mind, still thinking about how to get the musk. His mother will say to him, 'Tidy up the house a bit and let's have a good New Year's celebration. It has been several years since we last celebrated New Year's properly.'

"He will smile at his mother and reply, 'We can celebrate together every year, but the most important thing now is to treat your illness.' He will stay up all night caring for his mother.

"The next day, before dawn, he will remember there are musk deer in the mountain behind the village, but then he will also remember that it is a sacred mountain, and that the musk deer belong to the sacred mountain. Deities are inviolable. As he remembers that his father died violently because he tried to hunt a musk deer from the sacred mountain, a feeling of terror will assault him. His father's death due to his offense to the mountain gods will become the best example of karmic retribution. But when remembering his mother's illness, he will not feel frightened any more. He will think again about climbing up the mountain to kill the musk deer.

"Taking advantage of his mother's sleep, he will find his father's gun. Resolutely, he will head toward the back mountain with the gun on his shoulder. Almost at dawn on New Year's Day, the weather will still feel very cold. In spite of the cold, the village kids will be going door to door wishing everybody a happy New Year. He will know that New Year's Day is the most auspicious day of the year, a day when people should abstain from killing—let alone killing the livestock of the mountain deity. But he will feel he has no other choice at that moment, his only thought will be curing his mother's illness. His gun rocking back and forth on his shoulder, in the freezing morning wind, he will walk alone. That gun will already be full of rust spots, nothing of it shining any longer. When he puts two bullets into the barrel, it will sound as if it is going to break, but he will not doubt that gun at all. He will have complete faith that the gun will be able to kill a musk deer.

"When the sky becomes clear, he will arrive at the top of the mountain. At that moment, he will see a musk deer climbing not too far away and looking at him. He will squat quietly and aim his gun, but once again fear will attack his heart. Images of his father's violent death, as well as that black hole in his forehead, will clearly appear before his eyes. The arm holding the gun will tremble slightly. With his hand, he will vigorously clean his forehead, filled with beads of sweat. Exhaling a mouthful of air, he will put his weapon down, only to raise it up again after the frail and sick image of his mother's face appears before his eyes. He will hesitate, seeing alternatively the images of his father's tragic death and his mother's emaciated body. The sweat from his forehead will drip into his eyes, making his vision fuzzy. The sweat will make his palms so wet that he will not be able to grasp his weapon firmly. The long, muffled sound of a gun will be heard. Lengan will immediately think about death, feeling that he is surely dead and his soul is slowly flying to the other world. But he will soon realize he is not dead. He will touch his head and face and realize that he is still there. Lifting his head up instinctively, he will see a musk deer lying motionless on the hill not too far away from him. His eyes will look back at his gun, on the ground, parts of its frame scattered around. A strong smell of gunpowder will fill the air. He will pick up the broken pieces of the gun and look at them calmly for a while. With a sigh, he will say, 'Oh, gun, what kind of thing are you in the end? You indeed have such a formidable power!'"

Decho Zangpo, for a long time, had been bewildered by this story. He had entirely immersed himself in its atmosphere, to the point of forgetting completely about the repeated exhortations of Master Nāgārjuna, and all his sufferings with the failed trip attempts. And so he asked, "What the hell is a gun?"

After the Golden Corpse heard this, he said, "You poor devil! Your tongue slipped again!" And with a plop, he flew back to the Dewatsal cemetery.

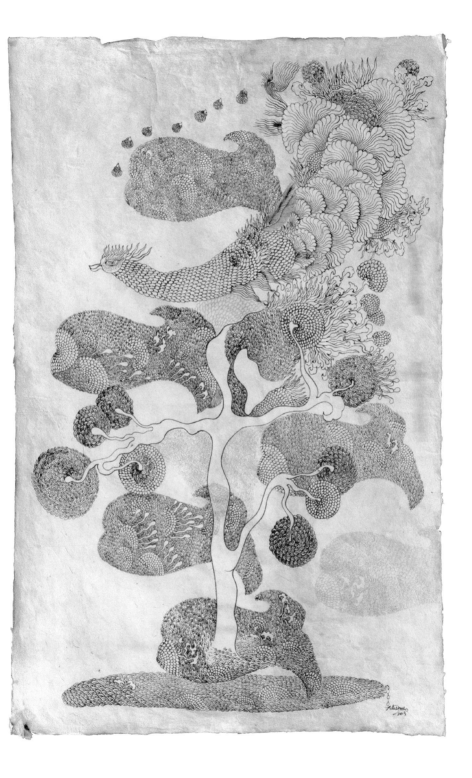

Wu Yao, *Wish-fulfilling Tree Series*

A SINGLE SHEET OF PAPER

Half of a blueish, rising sun appeared in a gap in the eastern mountains. He thought the blue-looking sun had risen slowly, but, oddly, no sooner had it risen than it set. Growing apprehensive, and now walking slowly, he came to a palace radiating a vivid, golden light and went in. Never had he seen anything like its shape and design, and he stared at the things inside the palace, eyes open in wonder. Eventually, his wide-open eyes fixed on a thick calendar hanging on the wall. Although he was now thirty years old, he had never in his life seen anything like this thick calendar. On the calendar it read, "32nd day of December in the year 2000." Seeing that, he stared, his mouth agape in astonishment. He looked at it one more time. There was no mistake. Clearly written on the calendar was "32nd day of December in the year 2000." As he stood there stunned, having no clue to what to do next, he saw a man come near. The man stared at him, devoid of any affection. Seeing the man's face, he trembled. The man, looking toward the calendar on the wall, said, "After seeing our calendar do you feel a sense of amazement?"

Hearing this, his head began to nod uncontrollably. The man continued, "Well now, there is no need to be amazed. Listen to what I have to say. This morning, the creator made us. Today, at daybreak, we came to this planet. That creator has made one hundred new people similar to me."

The man, explaining in this fashion, pointed out a corner of the palace. Looking in the direction the man was pointing, he saw that actually

Translated from the Tibetan by Michael Monhart. Originally published in *Literature from Tibet* (*Xizang wenxue*), no. 6 (2008). This short story was originally published in Chinese and later translated into Tibetan.

there were many people in groups, exchanging conversation with each other. They were all mostly in the shape and form of the man speaking to him. Now, not seeing the purpose of these new people, a suspicion arose in him.

The man continued, saying, "That creator went to another planet after he made us. I know the fate of these one hundred people: their past, present, and future. On this planet, we can only live for one hundred years. From now on, each year, one person will die. In this way, each year, the number of people will grow smaller and smaller, and in the end, the last death will be mine."

As they conversed, his confidence grew, and he questioned the man who was speaking. "You know the length of your life. Knowing this, don't you have suffering?"

The man's answer struck him as inconceivable.

"No, on the contrary, I think it's good."

"Why is that?"

"Our feelings, such as love, are already fixed, determined. You human beings are not able to grasp an understanding of that."

"If you say 'you human beings,' then what kind of people do you belong to?"

"Even I do not know what kind of people I belong to. However, we do not experience the sufferings of birth, sickness, old age, and death like humanity does. From birth to death, as now in the present, there is no change whatsoever in our outward appearances." As he thought about this, the man continued, staring at him. "I am someone who has mastered hundreds of kinds of expertise. However, I have the fault that, from the beginning, I have not known how to count. My only way to count is to take over counting after someone else has started. This morning, as I traveled to this planet, I saw that according to the calendar of your people, it is now the 31st day of December in the year 2000. We continued counting from the 31st to make our calendar. Today, in our world, it is the first day. What you see is the 32nd day of December in the year 2000. Are you still puzzled?"

He nodded as if to show he understood. The man then went on. "Inside the place where we live for one hundred years, on our calendar, it always says December in the year 2000. Each day, only the date increases, going up and up. In that way, one hundred years go on and on, longer than expected. That is how we come to the duration of our lives and our world."

The man stopped talking again and stared at him, a glimmer in his eyes, then continued. "This morning, I did some extensive research into things such as how humans are organized; however, the reference point we need is not there at all. Because of our inability to distinguish between men and women in these newly created one hundred people, we absolutely need a method of organization. However, what you call the cells of society, that is the family, cannot be realized. Because of that, we have to organize in our society only as individuals.

At that point, a doubt arose in his mind and he questioned the man, "If none of you can distinguish between men and women, how then do you live?"

The man continued his explanation with an attitude similar to before, "We each have our own place. We don't connect in any way to live together. We are a species devoid of love."

In response to this, he said, "Ah, you are what we humans call cold, devoid of love. However, on the surface, I don't see any differences whatsoever between you and us humans." He couldn't help laughing but quickly found a way to regain control.

The man replied, in a cold voice, "Yes, we have no love."

Seeing the way the conversation was now going, he tried another way of questioning the man. "Well, in that case, what kind of food do you rely on?"

Immediately, the man replied, saying carefully, "We are able to make a kind of nourishment that has the taste of this world's warm, muddy clay. This morning, the food we ate was muddy clay."

As he was saying this, the man took from an open box a finely shaped square piece of clay and, putting it into his mouth, started chewing it with savor. The man then took another square piece and, pushing it toward him, said, "Eat!" As soon as the man said, "Eat!" he asked himself why he felt so strange and wanted to avoid eating the clay. He could not bring himself to eat even a part of it.

The man, after he finished eating the square pieces of clay, picked up where he had left off, saying, "Our globe consists of one hundred flat, differently sized levels. Each year, after one person dies, the levels decrease by one. Our globe likewise grows smaller because the levels removed are the size of the dead person's food. After proceeding like this for one hundred years, that will be the day that I die, and our world will vanish from the universe without a trace. Now, because experts from your world are skilled at investigating the heavens, they can see there is an unusual planet in the universe. But investigate it as they like, any results will be inconclusive. Moreover, they can see that the planet is growing smaller every year, and that it vanishes after one hundred years. Don't get angry, this was new to me once. Our world, like yours, has its own orbit rotating around the sun."

At that time, a red moon rose slowly over the peak of the western mountains, and immediately the surroundings were covered in red moonlight. The man, glancing at the red moon rising, went on, "It is nighttime. For us also, it is time to rest." After hearing this explanation, the man took a step, intending to go away.

Suddenly, he grew angry and, thinking that the man had told his story to fool him, spoke in a loud, scolding voice, "Don't go like that! Go after you are finished listening to me. You're an animal without love. Who would believe this nonsense of yours? If there is no love in this world, it is impossible for anyone to live."

At that point, his wife gently woke him from his sleep and, puzzled, asked him, "Who were you scolding? You said I had no love? If I don't love you, how is it possible I can be your wife?"

Suddenly he sat up in the bed. He looked at his wife's face, his eyes motionless, unable to say anything at all. Then, in the morning sunlight, everything in the house became clear to him. The rays of sunlight, reflected in a mirror, directly illuminated the calendar on the wall. With eyes wide open, he focused on the calendar and saw the last single page. It clearly said the 31st of December in the year 2000. Suddenly he realized that day was yesterday. Stretching out his hand, he pulled away the last page. The spot where the calendar hung remained empty.

Ah! A new year begins. Also a new one hundred years.

GANG

1.

In Tibetan, *gang* means snow. It is also the name of a young girl found in the snow one evening twenty years ago by a shepherd named Chodpa.

That evening, Chodpa had dreamt that in the expanse of an empty universe, a woman, who seemed to be his wife, was hurriedly walking in a heavy snowfall holding a baby in her lap. In the broad reach of the sky, a clear, white moon rose and dazzling white snow appeared, with brilliant clarity, covering all the surrounding area. Even dim reflections were glittering. The four cardinal and four intermediate directions were quiet; however, the sobbing of a child could be heard continuously in the empty field. The shepherd Chodpa woke from sleep and thought, "Isn't that an illusion?" He shook his head strongly a few times, but the crying continued on as before, without stopping. Because the image of both a wife and a child had appeared so vividly to him in the dream, he chuckled involuntarily to himself, doubting that the sound could be real. Chodpa, having just reached the age of fifteen years old, not only hadn't thought about having a wife, but, even more so, had no idea who the woman and naked baby in the dream could be.

The crying could be heard without pause. As the shepherd Chodpa came out of his black yak-hair tent, he saw that, indeed, a lot of snow had fallen and, for a moment, he stood amazed. Across the sky, stars

Translated from the Tibetan by Michael Monhart. Originally published in *Light Rain* (*Sbrang char*), no. 2 (1999).

shimmered, and in the clear white light of the moon, this landscape of fallen snow had a beauty like he had never seen before. The shepherd could not help but be drawn to the sound of the cries, and after thinking a bit, he went quickly in the direction of the crying child. He clearly saw something shining brightly and immediately was afraid, powerless to take a step. But, after a brief moment, drawing from his own strength, his confidence returned, and he drew near to it, thinking, "Ah! That really is a child, a newborn naked baby."

Its entire body was white like snow and shone under the rays of the moon. Bending over, he thought, "When I look carefully, it is exactly like the child in the lap of the woman who appeared as my wife in the dream." At first he was afraid, but when he saw the genuine, now smiling, expression of the child, his fear diminished, and he felt a closeness to it. Holding it to his chest, he thought to bring the naked child inside, safe from the danger of the freezing cold. He loosened the strap of his robe, intending to put it into the front pocket. At that moment, however, again afraid and worried that it was an illusion, he put the child down, planning to go back to his tent.

When he calmed down a little, he thought, "I must look." While looking, he said to himself, "This truly is a person, not an illusion, and also very beautiful." Seeing it in that manner now, he was ashamed and regretted how he had almost run away. He thought, "If I abandon a newborn child like this in the snow, I will blame myself." Putting the child in the front pocket of his sheepskin robe, he went in the direction of his yak-hair tent. The child's body was actually transparent, crystal-clear on the inside and outside. He gazed inside the child, watching its organs moving with a slight, graceful movement, in time with the body's breath.

The baby found by the shepherd Chodpa was a girl. For days after, though he kept listening in all four cardinal directions, he did not hear any talk or rumors about a lost child. Likewise, no one came looking for her. So he decided he would care for her. As others would have various suspicions and might gossip about the child if they saw her transparent body, he made a very small sheepskin robe and wrapped her in it. He also thought it necessary that he give the child a name, but for the time being, he could not think of an appropriate one. One evening, several days later, by the light of the moon, he found the baby standing in the midst of the bright, very white snow. As soon as he saw her whole body emanating rays of light like snow, a thought vividly arose in his mind, "Gang. This name suits her perfectly."

The days passed steadily by, one by one. And because the woman often appeared in the world of the shepherd Chodpa's dreams, always as his wife, the feeling of missing her grew stronger each day.

2.

"When snow falls down and down
One remembers one's homeland"
—from a contemporary Tibetan song

Gang, staring at the girl singing songs on stage, stood transfixed. His mind was powerlessly drawn to the beautiful sound of her voice and tears swelled at the edges of his eyes. After a little time, all around, there was the sound of hands clapping. Even after the girl had finished her song and had come down, he continued to stare at the stage. His classmate Paljor, standing next to him and seeing this, had no idea what had come over his friend and said, in a low voice, "Gang, what's happened to you?" Gang, as if awakening from sleep, replied shyly, "It's nothing at all. Just now that song sent me back to my distant homeland. What is that girl's name?"

"Her name is also Gang," Paljor said. "She is a new student in the class this year. Actually, until now, I haven't paid her much attention, but looking closely, other than the usual differences between a man and a woman, your entire physical appearances and expressions are exactly alike. These days, this girl is the talk of everyone in the school. Everyone says that her body is white like snow. Some say that her body appears crystal-like, transparent." Paljor, while looking at Gang, continued, "So, the girls keep their distance from her. The boys, meanwhile, try to find any excuse, and do whatever possible, to be close to her. However, when she does not give the young boys as much as a sidelong glance, they become depressed. The girl really is white like snow, with a stunning beauty that the boys cannot get enough of."

Gang stared ahead, thinking. In a quiet voice, as if speaking to himself, he finally asked, "Gang. Is the girl's name really Gang?"

Paljor said, "It is. Her name is Gang."

When the evening assembly finished, the crowd poured out. As Gang was about to go, he tugged at Paljor and said, "You go first. I have to wait for her," then went alone in the direction of the stage. He saw her at the edge of the stage, about to go with some other girls. Coming up behind her, he tugged at her dress, saying, "Please wait. I would like to talk to you a little."

When he said this, the girl and those with her all turned and looked back. The other girls, in astonishment, shouted, "*At tshi!* How strange, how strange! The two are so similar!"

Even though a little anxiety arose in Gang's mind, he spontaneously felt a closeness towards the girl. She, having heard Gang speak, slowly turned around. As soon as she saw Gang's face, she trembled.

He asked her, "Is your name also Gang?"

"Yes, what of it?" she replied. As she now looked closely at him, she saw in front of her eyes a handsome young boy who appeared, as if in a mirror, no different from herself.

"My name is also Gang," he said. "My mind was drawn powerlessly to your song. When I listened to your song, I had the feeling of being back in my homeland far away. When our classmates talk like that, of us being so similar, it is like the two of us are twins at the chest of the same mother. Is that true? It really is like that." All this he said in one breath, clutching her hand tightly.

"This is a song I have kept in my heart for a long time," she said. "As I love the words and melody so much, I often secretly sing the song to myself. Singing the song, I too am powerless, missing my distant homeland. I feel a strong yearning to return and also a feeling of actually being back in my homeland." Staring at his face full of joy, she also relaxed, and the two suddenly found themselves outside, not even realizing they had left the gathering.

The snow that had been falling had now stopped. The moon shone, generously radiating rays of light in the middle of the stars. The snow-covered land was clear and brilliant.

The two, standing side by side in the snow, stared with one mind at the clear white moon, together admiring the view. In the moonlight, the snow was white and smooth; likewise, their faces were as white and smooth as the snow in the moonlight.

He spoke, "Gang, my distant homeland is at the foot of the snowy mountains. Not only is it a beautiful region, but that is also where my only relative lives, my kind mother."

And she replied, "Gang, my distant homeland, too, is at the foot of the snowy mountains. It also is a beautiful region. In that place, I have no other relatives except for my father."

3.

From that time forward, the two were as a body and its shadow. Their classmates and teachers said the two were like twins and, for quite a while, they were the main topic of conversation.

After taking the midterm examination, each of the two sent a letter home, writing that in their class there was someone with the same name, and that, among their classmates, they were regarded as twins. The two were also close in their support for each other, and each asked their parent to, by all means, please visit.

One afternoon, fifteen days after they had sent the messages, the father and mother, spontaneously, without any previous discussion between them, arrived at the classroom at the same time. At first, as the two met face to face, they did not move in the least, staring at each other. After a moment had passed, tears ran down from their eyes, and without hesitation, they hugged each other close. Chodpa, the shepherd, very moved, said, "Are you not the person I have waited for in my dreams for some twenty years?"

The woman, also moved, wiped away tears as she cried, unable to catch her breath, "I, too, for twenty years have waited in the depths of my heart for you."

Gang and Gang, having seen this and not knowing quite what to make of it, said together, "Father, Mother, what has happened?" The two adults, only then, as if they were awakening from sleep, stared at the faces of the boy and girl and said with one voice, "Ah, ah, the two are so alike."

Chodpa then said, "Girl, it is good for you to know your story now. I found you in the snow, one moonlit night some twenty years ago. Who you were, and who your mother and father were, I myself did not even know. Later, as you were like snow itself, I gave you that name." After a moment, Chodpa then explained in detail all that had happened.

At the same time, the woman who had appeared in Chodpa's dream as his wife also explained, "Boy, the time has come for you to know everything. One moonlit night, some twenty years ago, I found you in the snow. I didn't know who you were or who your mother and father were. Afterwards, as you were like the snow, I gave you that name." The sequence of events was the same as that of Chodpa finding the girl.

They both continued at the same time, "From the time you both were young, even though you asked again and again about whether you had a father or mother, we replied, 'What is the use of so many questions? When you are grown up, it will be possible to know all.'"

Now that the twenty-year-old secret was released, Gang and Gang were full of feelings of joy and sorrow mixed together. Kneeling on the ground, they said, "You both are really our kind father and mother. We two are also children of your hearts." When they prostrated, saying this, tears fell from the eyes of the shepherd Chodpa and the woman who had appeared as his wife in his dreams, and they embraced the boy and girl.

4.

Gang and Gang's four years as students at the college passed quickly. When they reached the end of their studies, the two, passing up an opportunity to stay in the city, returned to the grasslands of their childhoods.

After having met face to face with Chodpa in the school, Gang's mother then moved to be with him. The two, who had waited and longed for each other for some twenty years, bound in love, now lived happily together. Because Gang and Gang were also now with them, their aim to enjoy life together came true. In that small family of wife, husband, and the two young ones, the sounds of laughter filled the air.

Gang and Gang were appointed to work at the elementary school in the grasslands and felt how wonderful it was to stay with the children, doing whatever was needed for their happiness and well-being.

One day at the beginning of winter, when one could not see even a cloud in the openness of the clear sky, Gang was teaching a language lesson to some of the elementary school students. When she wrote in large letters on the blackboard the syllables *kha wa*,* a feeling came to her like all of her bodily energy was used up. More than ten minutes were needed to write the two syllables. Suddenly, she became very dizzy, and her mind dimmed. After a moment, her consciousness gradually returned, and her mind cleared. "*Kha wa, kha wa,*" she said, beginning to teach. At that time there was a young girl in the class who was fond of asking questions. She stood up and asked in a low, humble tone, "Teacher, what is the meaning of *kha wa?*"

---

* *Kha wa* is another word for snow in Tibetan.

"That . . . that. . . ." For a moment, Gang could not give an answer to the girl. Normally, that would have been a usual question; however, today, because she did not know the answer, her face turned red, and she did not know what to do. Some students shouted, "It's snowing! It's snowing!"

Outside, snow really was falling. It was the first snowfall of the winter. Gang and Gang had waited a long time in the depths of their hearts for this snow. Gang did not say anything, and she went outside the classroom. At the same time, in another classroom, Gang was also teaching, and he, too, ran outside. The two stood side by side staring at the pure snowflakes falling down, unable to stop smiling. Gang's eyes suddenly flashed, and she said over and over in a high voice, "Snow, this is snow." The children also came outside. Jumping and playing in the snow that floated through the sky and above the ground, they cried, "Oh, snow!" Gang and Gang both joined in the children's play, and the clear sound of laughing swirled through the sky like the falling snow.

5.

Three years had passed since Gang and Gang had come to the grasslands. In the winter, because heavy snowfalls had occurred one after another on the grasslands, the hay and straw for the animals were covered and pushed down by snow. When spring came, time for the fields to come back to life, the grass still had not sprouted. Many of the nomads' livestock died and everyone became depressed and anxious. Until now, the people had not faced such a serious problem due to snowstorms. The community gathered for a meeting to decide how to quickly help their domestic animals.

On that day, there was an agitated crowd at the newly built athletic field. In the middle of the crowd, the old and new village leaders moved about, waving and gesturing, talking to the people. Feeling discouraged, the crowd surrounding them bowed their heads to their chests in despair.

They had all met for a half a day, but because they came to no conclusion, their gathering was in vain, and the meeting broke up. The people, having lost hope, were about to go. Gang and Gang looked at them with open, caring eyes and said, "Don't be downcast. We will plan everything." When they said these consoling words, everyone thought that, since even the old and new village leaders had no idea what to do, what possible plan could two elementary teachers have? And thinking such, they returned to their homes.

In fact, the two were thinking that, in order to help the community, they would offer to exhibit their transparent bodies to the public for money. Gang said to Gang, "We two will work hard together. But, you don't have to exhibit. It is enough that you support me." Gang, nodding her head, agreed.

The next day, the two wrote a letter to their friend and former classmate Paljor, now a reporter at the provincial newspaper. They clearly discussed the situation of the nomad region and their plan.

After a week, the letter the two had sent came to Paljor. At first he could not believe it. When he was a student, he had heard rumors of Gang and Gang's transparent bodies. Figuring that if it were true back then, it would still be uniquely valuable news now, he showed the letter to the chief editor saying, "I would like to go to the grasslands for an interview." The editor looked at the letter a few more times, and even though he could not believe it, because Paljor asked again and again, the chief editor begrudgingly let him go.

Going by public bus, the reporter Paljor arrived first at the county seat in a remote area of the province. From the county seat, he went a further three days on foot and at last arrived in the nomad region where Gang and Gang lived. After seeing in all directions the dead animals and sad conditions of the grasslands, he had a heavy feeling and, at the same time, was deeply moved by the unselfish behavior and actions of Gang and Gang.

After the reporter Paljor had written up the news, it became a hot topic in his department at the provincial newspaper. Soon, many reporters from both near and far came swirling like bees from the four cardinal and four intermediate directions and assembled at Gang and Gang's place. They took many pictures of Gang's wondrous body, which they used to illustrate the articles they wrote about this unusual event and place in the world. Because of the publicity, Gang and Gang were, in a short time, the talk of many inside and outside the country.

Along with the publicity, in the town of Gang and Gang, there was a change, as if the world had been turned upside down. At first, except for few people, there was no one who came to that place. Gradually, there were more and more visitors of different nationalities, from cities and towns all over the country as well as foreign countries. The people coming to view Gang's transparent body filled the area surrounding the school like an anthill being opened. As for the kinds of people gathering, there were merchants with various types of goods, singers with good voices, skilled dancers, and even fortune-tellers and astrologers purporting to know everything about everything. All came of their own accord and were earnest in their work. What was before a remote, quiet grassland area swelled into an ocean of milling people and waves of dust, becoming like the small market in a city. The visitors' discarded fruit rinds, cigarette packs, empty liquor bottles, and so forth filled the area of the grassy plain around the clock.

In the daytime, because it was necessary to provide a welcome for all the visitors who came to the exhibition, Gang and Gang did not have the time to relax, or to even take a tea break. When evening came, at last having the opportunity to recover a little, they taught, and after teaching, counted the income from the day.

After about half a month of selling tickets to the exhibit of Gang's body, they were able to amass a large amount of money. The two gave all the money to the village chief. All the young boys of the community were sent to work and, having bought flour, barley, rice, fodder, tools, and so forth in the county seat, they brought everything back to their village. After a little while, all the people and cattle were released from the torment of their hunger and their suffering under the hand of the lord of death.

After about a month, some foreigners arrived. Through their translators, they expressed their wish to examine in detail and take photos of Gang's transparent body. As he was able to fulfill their wish, the two were again able to acquire a large amount of money.

Then the foreigners learned that the woman, Gang, who was collecting the money, also had a transparent body. They said they would pay as much as necessary if they could take photos of the two together. However, as Gang and Gang would not agree to be photographed together, the foreigners, growing desperate, went to the village chief. They pleaded with him but got nowhere.

The foreigners, for the sake of accomplishing their goal, bought some black-hair yak tents and took up residence. Going to the village chief again and again, they kept increasing the amount of money they offered. Through those discussions, they came to know the situation of the grassland people.

Although initially there were complaints about the outsiders, the people of the village, their palms itching, thought they could get even more money if they fulfilled the wishes of the foreigners and secretly criticized Gang and Gang. Even though the village chief did not initially go along with the thinking of the villagers, gradually his palms also began to itch, and wanting more money, he too began to criticize Gang and Gang. From time to time, one or two people would come to talk to Gang and Gang, but it was impossible to change the siblings' minds. Finally, the helpless foreigners bribed government officials to use their power on the village chief. The village chief, though wanting money, was afraid of Gang and Gang's father and mother and had absolutely promised them not to agree to give in. The foreigners were thus not able to achieve their goal.

In the absolute darkness of an evening, as when a thief comes to hide, the government officials, becoming desperate, gathered together with the village chief for a final meeting. They decided that the next day, if Gang and Gang did not allow the photos, then they would forcefully take the pictures.

That very evening, the government officials, the village leaders, and others from the grassland all together had a similar dream. In the dream, an old man with hair and a beard white like a conch shell, wrathfully said, "Gang and Gang are children of the snow mountains. It is not right to be ungrateful to them."

Likewise, at the same time, a dream also came to the shepherd Chodpa and his wife. In the dream, an old man with hair and beard white like a conch shell said, "Gang and Gang are children of the snow mountains. Because their final dwelling place is in the snow mountains, it is time for them to come back in that direction. I ask this kindly, from the bottom of my heart." Smiling, he disappeared.

The next day, as soon as it was daybreak, the people milled about, agitated. They gathered together in one place and talked about the amazing dream of the previous night. The shepherd Chodpa and his wife stood in an icy wind, staring into the distance at the majestic white mountains. Although they knew clearly that Gang and Gang had left for the distant snow-covered mountains, there was not even a little bit of sadness in their hearts. They knew it was Gang and Gang's final dwelling place.

The people also, standing near Chodpa and his wife, left behind their thoughts and criticisms and stood staring at the distant, majestic, white mountains.

THE DOCTOR

1.

The day has broken. The river is flowing unceasingly. A few leaves grow from the young tree recently planted by the riverbank. The spring air is still a little cold, and an icy wind blows unceasingly.

The sun slowly rises from the east. Man A and Woman A crouch by the young tree and gaze at the leaves that grow on the trunk.

Man A says, without blinking, "It's only been a few days since this tree was planted, but its leaves are already growing. How strong the vital force is!"

Woman A, without blinking an eye either, replies, "The vital force will undergo birth, old age, and death, like this tree. When one thinks about it, human life is totally absurd."

Man A sighs deeply and says, "Human beings are just like trees. Upon reflection, it is completely absurd."

Woman A also sighs deeply, "The world and *samsara* are utterly meaningless."

Translated from the Tibetan by Françoise Robin. Originally published in *Art of the Masses* (*Mang tshogs sgyu rtsal*), no. 4 (2003). English translation originally published in *Himalaya, the Journal of the Association for Nepal and Himalayan Studies*, 33, no. 1 (March 2014): 90–96.

Man A says, with a wise air about him, "But the difference between the two is that human beings have faith and trees don't."

Woman A says, nodding her head, "Right. With faith in the Three Jewels, life force acquires a meaning, despite its impermanence."

Man A and Woman A, hands joined, pray, "I take refuge in the Three Jewels."

Man A and Woman A get up and scrutinize the opposite bank of the river. The boatman there is looking back at them.

Man A, upon seeing the boatman, calls out, "Hey! What have you seen?"

The boatman replies in a loud voice, "Nothing, I haven't seen a thing."

Woman A, too, calls out to him, "Pray tell, watch carefully! The doctor is about to come."

The boatman turns around. He glances and looks back at them. He shouts, "No, I cannot see anything."

Man A and Woman A sit again by the tree. Man A sighs and says, "If the doctor does not come on time, it will be extremely serious."

Woman A, sighing too, said, "He's about to come. It has been over one month since we sent him an invitation letter."

Man A says, sighing ceaselessly, "One fourth of the inhabitants of our Earth community have been stricken by *mnemokleptia*, and the disease is still spreading. It's really terrifying."

Woman A stops sighing, "By the Three Jewels! Will the doctor be able to cure this disease?"

Man A's face instantly expresses confidence as he says, "There have been doctors in the human world for two millennia, people say. It is also said that an epidemic of *mnemokleptia* strikes human beings once every century. Doctors have acquired excellent expertise in this field, so we can trust them completely."

Having thus spoken, Man A looks at the opposite bank of the river, still with a confident look on his face.

Woman A stretches and says, "I pray for the doctor to arrive on time."

A din can be heard in the distance. Man A and Woman A turn around to look at where the noise is coming from. A vehicle appears and stops near them. The vehicle is wrapped in the dust that it raises. After the dust has settled, several people get out, whispering to each other.

One of them comes nearer and tells Man A and Woman A, "We come from the Sun community, of which I am the head. We flee because we fear that our community will be contaminated by *mnemokleptia*, on account of your community."

Man A asks, astonished, "What? You are from the Sun community? Why have I never heard of it?"

The man replies, with a distant air, "It is because you have not seen much in life. Tell me the truth: how can we cross the river? If you help us, we'll let you have our vehicle."

Woman A asks nervously, "Do you really mean what you're saying? If you do, we'll help you."

The men say, nodding their heads, "Yes, it is true, it is true. This beat-up car is of no use to us anymore."

Man A and Woman A wave their arms to call to the boatman who is on the other side of the river.

The boatman comes closer slowly, rowing his boat. The men, once on board, order, "Go, quickly!"

The boatman glances at Man A and Woman A and says anxiously, "So many people on board one single boat. This is very dangerous."

But the men, without the slightest hesitation, say, "It is even more dangerous to stay here. Hurry up."

The boatman prays "By the Three Jewels!" and starts rowing towards the opposite bank. When they are about to reach it, one man falls into the water, but the others do not pay attention. They just gaze, eyes wide open, at the body being carried away by the current.

Once they have reached the other side, the men say, "Sacrificing one individual or two for the sake of the group is fine."

The boatman, upon hearing this, is agape, eyes goggled.

2.

The heat in the heart of summer is intense. The tree trunk and its branches have fully grown, and its leaves are about to shrivel in the midday heat. The river bed has dried up; its stones shine brightly.

The faces of Man A and Woman A are emaciated and cracked. It seems both have aged a little.

The man swiftly wipes the sweat from his face and says, "What heat! I would never have thought I could experience such agony. Better to die than to live like this."

Woman A also swiftly wipes the sweat from her face and says, "Have you never heard the phrase 'There is no happiness whatsoever in *samsara*, which is like the tip of a needle?' In *samsara*, everyone ineluctably experiences suffering. Without that, they could not feel the urge to grow."

Man A says, waving his arms, as if he had not heard, "By the Three Jewels! By the Three Jewels! I cannot stand it any longer. Better to die quickly than to undergo such agony!"

Woman A says, with a sneer, "Aren't you driving the Three Jewels toward something evil by saying such things? You are a breathing being. Could the Three Jewels, who cultivate love and compassion, make you die?"

At that moment, Man B, of the Earth community, runs towards them and says, out of breath, "Everything's going wrong. Everything's going wrong. *Mnemokleptia* has contaminated half of our community. Something terrible is in store."

Man A says, fidgeting, "Alas! What to do? Why hasn't the doctor arrived yet?"

Woman A, concerned, says, "As long as the doctor does arrive, it is fine. We have been waiting for him here for the whole spring. What bothers me is that I still have some little things to do at home."

Man A joins the palms of his hands. "By the Three Jewels! By the Three Jewels! May the doctor be here soon."

A tractor, in a racket, comes near the tree. Man A asks the driver, "Where are you from? Where are you heading?"

The driver replies, reluctantly, "We come from the Moon community. We flee because we fear that the *mnemokleptia* that strikes your Earth community will contaminate us in our turn."

The driver presses strongly on the accelerator and moves straight ahead from the river bank. Blue smoke rises from behind the vehicle.

Woman A says, "These people are amazing. Don't they know that the doctor is due to come? What kind of an escape can be expected by fleeing like this?"

3.

The autumn wind blows fiercely. The withered leaves on the full-grown branches of the tree are falling. Man A's forehead, and that of Man B, and that of Woman A, are wrinkled, and all look weary. The afternoon sun shines horizontally into their faces.

Suddenly, the sky is shrouded in dark clouds and a violent rain falls. Man A, Man B, and Woman A take shelter under the tree.

A torrential rain keeps falling. Another woman, Woman B, runs towards the tree. Her clothes are soaked by the rain, making her shiver.

With a trembling face, she says, "All is lost, all is lost. Three quarters of our community have been affected by *mnemokleptia*. And the toll keeps rising."

Woman A takes Woman B by the hand and tells her, "By the Three Jewels! My parents, my siblings, my husband, and my children are still there. May the Three Jewels protect them!"

Woman B says, her face still trembling, "Some cases of incest between parents and children, and between brothers and sisters, are happening in the community. Try as we might, we cannot prevent them. It is really terrifying."

Man A says, worriedly, "We have no option but to wait for the doctor. We have no choice."

Man B sighs and says, "But, that so-called 'doctor,' does he really exist after all? We have been waiting for him for two seasons without seeing as much as his shadow. Sometimes, I lose faith in him."

"We have no other option but to wait for him. He will be able to cure this disease. But we are helpless."

They leave the tree and call the boatman by his name. He is on the other side of the river and does not hear, as a strong rain keeps falling. He scrutinizes the distance, totally motionless.

A hand-driven tractor, coming from nowhere, arrives at their side. A few men get down and mutter loudly while kicking it. "This heap of junk cannot outdo a man when it comes to driving in the mud. For sure, driving it is out of the question any longer."

Man A asks them, "What is your community? I have the feeling that I have never met you before."

They reply, "We come from the Star community. We flee because we fear that the *mnemokleptia* that is striking your community may contaminate us. In times of need, this heap of junk is more useless than a human being."

Seeing that they are about to leave, Woman B asks them, "If you are going to flee, would you consider giving us your tractor? We badly need it."

135

They say, "Take it, take it! We didn't know how to get rid of it," then try to head towards the river bank.

Man A stands in their way and warns them, "The river is big now. If you venture there, there is a great danger that it will carry you away."

They say, "Let it carry us away! We have no intention whatsoever to stay here anyway."

Without heeding Man A's warning, they go ahead. Upon reaching the middle of the river bed, the current carries them away. No trace of them is left.

When Man A, Man B, Woman A, and Woman B see this, their mouths agape, eyes fixed, they say, "It really is terrifying."

4.

It is a freezing winter. The tree branches have grown in all directions, a pitiful sight. As the sun is about to disappear behind the mountains in the west, the sunset rays shine on the creased faces of Man A, Man B, Woman A, and Woman B. The river has frozen into a thick layer of ice. The four of them, their necks stretched, are looking towards the opposite bank.

After a long time, they circle the old tree and make small talk.

"We are old now, like this tree. Our bodies will certainly not be able to bear such cold weather."

"By the Three Jewels! Down in this world, we have no option but waiting. I might as well die now. I do not feel any longer like waiting for this doctor who is not coming anyway."

Man B asks, with a sigh, "Don't human beings spend their life waiting for something? But waiting for what, nobody knows. We have never seen this so-called 'doctor,' so how could we know what we are waiting for?"

Woman B, contrary to the other three, does not sigh when she says, "If you do not know what to expect, why wait then?"

The boatman's eyes still look carefully into the distance.

Man A sees his wife run towards him. He steps forward to welcome her.

Man A's wife stares at his face, as if she has lost something, and asks him, "Who are you?"

The gaze of Man A becomes blurred, as if he too has lost something. He steps forward and asks Woman A, "Who are you?"

The gaze of Woman A, too, becomes blurred. She steps forward and asks Man B, "Who are you?"

The gaze of Man B, too, becomes blurred. He steps forward and asks Woman B, "Who are you?"

The boatman then shouts in their direction, "The doctor has arrived! The doctor has arrived!"

The doctor, followed by the boatman, runs in their direction, walking on the frozen river.

The gaze of Woman B becomes blurred. She asks the boatman, looking at him, "Who are you?"

The gaze of the boatman becomes blurred too. He turns around, glances at the doctor and asks him, "Who are you?"

The gaze of the doctor becomes blurred, as if he has lost something. He reflects for a while, examines himself carefully, and asks, "Who am I?"

Wu Yao, *The Song of Wishes*

ABOUT THE TRANSLATORS

Michael Monhart (MA, STM, LP) earned a Master's degree in Ethnomusicology from the University of Washington, and a Master's degree in Tibetan Studies from Columbia University. He has done fieldwork in Tibetan monasteries in Nepal, and published and lectured widely on Tibetan ritual music. He is a Jungian psychoanalyst in private practice in New York.

Carl Robertson (Ph.D., University of Oregon) is Associate Professor of Chinese at Southwestern University. His research interests include late imperial (Ming-Qing) fiction, Chinese-language pedagogy, Chinese religion, comparative modernisms, and lyric theory and narratology.

Françoise Robin (Ph.D., INALCO) teaches Tibetan Language and Literature at the Institut national des langues et civilisations orientales (INALCO) in Paris. She is one of the most prominent scholars of Tibetophone literature and film, and an accomplished and prolific translator of modern Tibetan literature. In 2014, together with Brigitte Duzan, she published the first collection of French translations of Pema Tseden's short stories (*Neige*, Philippe Picquier 2013).

Patricia Schiaffini-Vedani (Ph.D., University of Pennsylvania) is one of the pioneers in the study of Sinophone Tibetan Literature. Her volume *Modern Tibetan Literature and Social Change*, coedited with Lauren Hartley, was published by Duke University Press in 2008. She currently teaches Chinese language, as well as China and Tibet related courses, at Texas State University in San Marcos (TX). Dr. Schiaffini is also the President and Founder of Tibetan Arts and Literature Initiative, an NGO devoted to training Tibetan teachers and promoting Tibetan-language education and literacy in China.

ABOUT THE ARTIST

Wu Yao is the artistic name of Karma Dorje Tsering (b.1963), a Tibetan artist from Yushu (Qinghai province). He is the winner of prestigious Chinese art and book illustration prizes. He currently lives in Beijing where he works as book designer for the Beijing Nationalities Publishing House.